Waiting for you to speak

the winning poems
of the 1998
Sandburg-Livesay Anthology
Contest

judged by
Jim C. Wilson

UnMon America
Pittsburgh, 1999

Library of Congress Cataloging-in-Publication Data

Waiting for you to speak : the winning poems of the 1998 Sandburg-
    Livesay Contest / judged by Jim C. Wilson.

     p.   cm.
    ISBN 1-884206-05-0
    1. American poetry — 20th century. 2. Canadian poetry —
20th century. 3. English poetry — 20th century. I. Wilson, Jim C.
II. Sandburg-Livesay Anthology Contest.

PS615.W27   1999   99-39567
811'.5408 — dc21   CIP

The quotation from Ralph Waldo Emerson is from *The Journals of Ralph Waldo Emerson, Volume V* (Boston: Houghton, Mifflin and Company, 1909–1914).

UnMon America

(a division of Unfinished Monument Press)
PO Box 4279
Pittsburgh, PA
15203

Unfinished Monument Press is a subsidiary of
Mekler & Deahl, Publishers
meklerdeahl@globalserve.net
www.meklerdeahl.com
905-312-1779

Cover illustration: Gilda Mekler
Design by Gilda Mekler
Film by SE Graphics
Printing by Transcontinental

Table of Contents

Peggy Poole

First Prize

Sentences

Why did we drive home that day in silence
as though we hadn't heard the specialist's sentence?
It might have been an ordinary outing
or a visit to a friend some miles away.
My mind keeps vivid details of that journey
the trees full-leafed, the sudden right-hand turn.
I gripped the wheel, waiting for you to speak
but you stared at the beacon on the skyline
which for decades has guided sailors home.
Half-way back, I could pretend no longer;
watching the road ahead I chose the words:
'You don't do things by halves, my dear, do you?'
My voice was set against the engine's droning
but quietly you managed then to answer
'It's more or less what I had expected.'
And that was it. The rest, to quote, is silence.

Respite

From the moment I reached up
to pick the first raspberry
calm caressed me, and his cancer
which was calling daughters home
gave way to childhood memories —
picking cherries, raspberries,
hiding in fruit bushes,
escaping . . .

Each tiny red globule
gave promise of an easy gourmet meal
for people, shocked and anxious,
whose appetites were left
in Geneva, London, Bristol.

Today, one year later,
in the same fruit garden
I pick raspberries again; this time
they'll grace a table for one.

Gillian Harding-Russell

SECOND PRIZE

I wear my mother's bones

(on fracturing my pelvis, soon after my mother's death)

like bracelets, inside ribs
xylophone with one more note
passed mother to daughter — jingle jangle
in my blood as I breathe in

out

live inside this rigid cage with swollen bars,
my mother's bones   live between these hips
this whirlpool, through pelvic cavity

eclipse — violin with invisible strings
jingle jangle under the gurgle
of blood, wet life

blood-stream over rocks. I wear
my mother's bones like bracelets, bangles.
She enters through the doorknobs
of my knees, shines a flashlight

ice cold down the corridor of my thighs.
I hear her in my windpipe, her voice suddenly
my voice, querulous
may surprise me and my listeners.

A silent tune whistles up
and down my spine, whines
in my blood, my mind
shrills my waiting brain, the house

where I spend the night, crosswind
of my dreams winnowing through.
I hear her jingle jangle, bangles,
bracelets everywhere —

in my bones, my blood, my brain,
behind my eye, the left eye
unknowing what the right eye
knows
through crystal cornea, dust motes
sunspots internal interferences, clouds
straight ahead.

I hear my mother's bones
in wind chimes through glass windows — the aeolian harp
my father loved and talked about and loved,

we transported from beside the purple martin feeder
and the blue spruce outside
their home, pointing tall

out of earth. The chimes, they jingle
jangle in my bones with their hinged knees,
beseeching elbows, dancing in an unseen wind,

its count so catchy, hard
to catch. In the air
above ourselves, the trees, the earth

they jingle jangle

to the stars

Joan Poulson

Last Day

After his burial
being in this snow-dumpling village,
coiled cat in the oxbow of a river,
is like lying with a lover
certain he won't check the clock.

Snowflakes big as a baby's fist
soften the mill's outline.
I take the track up the Wend,
whistle for Sam.

Families are out with sledges.
Laughter on the wind.
It's an easterly.

Alone on the hill, wind's voice clearer
under surface snow,
lifting it to smoke towards the moor.

Behind us the sky smoulders.
A grief of rooks
in the glittery meadow by the river.

The wind boils, lining up snow and earth.

I swirl at a movement — only a haze
of contorted trees
but Sam, snow-muzzled, points.

It's the last day of the year.
The sun's being swallowed.
I yell his name, run for home.

Alice B. Toklas Cooks Fish

My grandmother insisted that 'once caught
fish should have nothing more to do with water'.

When Picasso came to lunch I simmered
dry white wine with blade mace,
a leaf from Apollo's laurel and herbs:
thyme, tarragon, rosemary, fresh torn;
earth and sun resonating through my body . . .

Later I laid a firm striped bass to poach,
removed it from the fire,
left it to cool in the *court bouillon*.

My design was inspired — satin coverlet
of yellow mayonnaise: eggs, green oil.
To amuse, with a pastry tube, swirled
an extravagance of red cream,
not tainted with commercial colouring
but from my own paste
— tomatoes lusciously plumped with sun.
And then cunning detail:
sieved hard-boiled eggs, whites, yolks
kept separate and truffles finely sliced.
A final touch — dusting of *fines herbes*
with . . . my own conceit . . . basil.
I was proud of my chef d'oeuvre.

'Incroyable!' Picasso exclaimed
as Helene brought it to table
but Gertrude rocked in silent mirth
when, inflection of eyebrow perfect-pitched
that one murmured that it might rather
have been sculpted in honour of Matisse.

Susan Ioannou

HONOURABLE MENTION

Kosovo

An eye for an eye is claw justice
— but two from this shivering Muslim woman?

What triumph bleeds
from severing both her ears?

Hack off any thief's wrist,
but why, one by one, her innocent fingers?

Not even a trophy hunter
gouges out the nose.

Like meat unhooked,
roll her whimpering down the woods.

A day later, laugh at the shots
— war's lowest form of mercy.

Srebrenica Suite

1. Bombed

In the blown-out wall
midnight's dragonflies

rise with sparks
to blacken the moon.

2. To a Bride of War

I lay the lilies of hate, my love,
along your bloodied hair.
From twisted foot and crumpled dress
the blue bruise crawling up your cheek
collapses a last breath.
May long white petals perfume your death.

Rubble is your marriage bed.
Blackened beams let in the sky.
Frost fills an emptied shoe.

Sleep quiet
though new thunder splits
this battered rock, and air bursts red.

I lay these lilies by your head
to wed you with old earth.

➤

3. The Abandoned Hospital

Bone-withered,
their eyes are like peeled eggs
turning black, and back
inside half-emptied skulls.

Fingers, red lumps puffed with cold,
cannot hold even tatters
over transparent skin.

Pieces of selves, not people,
their fireworked nerves shudder.
Above, the fractured moon
dangles its sparking cord.

4. Survivor

Each night,
a black-scarfed woman
squats by the riverbank.

Her small net
splashes and crawls
— a boot? a bone?

Behind,
barbed wire
catches the moon.

5. After the Raid

No clear deep pool
where pebbles shiver
but a looking glass steamed over

her face floats up nothing.

6. Torturer

We expect a face
that could splinter mirrors:
nose, a long interrogation point,
eyes, sharpened skewers,
mouth, a red sneer,

but after shrieks' steel in the bone,
not his casual turning away,
the half-hidden yawn.

Becky D. Alexander

Down the Road

I heard about this guy,
a working stiff for the Roads Department,
picked up his pay every Thursday,
took it home to his faceless wife.

On time,
no complaints,
ate his lunch by the lunchroom clock.

Until the day he bumped into the foreman,
made that pompous ass wear coffee.
Tempers lost.
Fired on the spot.

Collected his lunch pail,
punched the clock,
headed out to the vehicle bay.
Got himself a road liner.
Hopped aboard —
drove off down the road,
setting those lines every which way:
up, down, sideways, zigzags, dots,
and sometimes around
in tight little circles.
Good thing he couldn't get the damned thing to spell.

Left the machine dry and empty, his mark on the road.
Took five men three weeks to cover his tracks.

Winona Baker

Swimming Toward an Island

We never broke step
When we crossed the bridge

with one useless arm
we swim
toward the island

We tread water
when we can no longer swim
Someone in a coracle
a cedar dug-out canoe
may come along

believe that
believe
there is an island

Jackie Bartley

The Place No One Returns From

The year we were married
they uncovered the Qin
Emperor's terracotta army,

7,000 soldiers and horses
frozen as if in readiness
to march into battle

with an enemy fierce enough
to frighten them to life
as they accompanied the emperor

into an afterlife he must
have dreaded. At the end
of our first summer together,

we spent a day at the local
county fair where, inside a tent,
away from the sun's terrible heat,

we heard a radio announcement from
the President of the United States:
the pullout of troops

from Vietnam, a place no one
we knew had ever returned from.
But no one else in the tent

seemed to hear. They shuffled
as if in a funeral procession
past the pens of 4H livestock,

the black-faced sheep, huge
bristling hogs, the Herefords
with their wide, reproachful eyes,

the ghostly Charolais. The men
rubbed their stubbled chins.
The women hoisted toddlers up

onto their hips. Outside,
we rode the Tilt-A-Whirl,
ate Italian sausage bathed

in fried peppers and onions,
sipped our colas and waited
in line for the Ferris wheel.

Our goal, to be at the top
precisely at sunset,
to watch the bald sun simmer

in a haze of fair dust
and smog from nearby mills,
mills about to go

belly-up, the valley strewn
with their huge metal carcasses
rusting beside rivers

like the discarded armor
of a perished battalion
waiting for us, the living,

to discover and utter
right words for peaceful
release.

Saw Mill in Dry Creek Canyon

From her raspberry patch, Ada hears robins chattering,
her husband at his work, the familiar high-pitched whine
sharp saw teeth make biting bark from logs.

Jim squares two sides of a log so thick through
it hits him chest high. With cant hook impaled,
he strains to turn the log, as heavy as a box car
of freshly cut wood. He doesn't notice

his frayed jeans so close to moving parts.
Frayed ends catch, pull his pants leg tight,
jam his right leg into the whirring blade.
His booted foot, nearly to his knee, drops
between carriage parts.

                    Blood spurts,
a fountain of wine, discoloring log, saw, machinery.
Jim grabs his stubbed-off leg. Blood, thin like wine,
oozes through. He pulls off his belt, secures it
around the stub.

Ada, sensing something amiss, looks up, hears
the robin's chirrup above the creek's roar, no whine of saw.
Pulled toward the mill, she hears Jim's frantic call.

She gasps in air, pulls her fresh apron off, folds it
against raw flesh. Her skirt darkens as she helps
Jim inside. She places a folded sheet across the wound,
tears another for a tourniquet. The sheet crimsons
as red as raspberries just picked. She cranks
the black two-piece phone.

Years later, neither Jim nor Ada speaks of that day,
how she retrieved his lifeless foot, removed the shoe,
            or of all their tears
that would not change a thing.

Marion Beck

Manchurian Elm in Winter

It is a witch of a tree
all angles, knots and gnarls
with limbs thrust skyward in a curse
the epitome of harshness
such ugliness would not be tolerated
in other places
but here where every tree is planted
cosseted like a sickly child
measured for growth
girdled each spring against the worm
admired for every scanty leaf or bloom
it represents a triumph
reminds us of other tougher times
and cuts us down
to size

Margaret Behr

Tom's Will

All
blood and bone,
flesh,
now still.

The mourners scatter.
Skin, cell and vein,
the cold tissues,
committed to fire,
rise into air.

What's left of a body
after fire:
the long bones,
skull and spine,
ground to dust.

I hold in an urn
nine pounds of ash
that was a living man.

Tom said:
add the ash
to earth and water,
make a clay.

The potter whispers,
fingers and moulds,
and the pots rise
flaring
out from the centre
of the turning wheel.

Dried and fired,
on the plain brown sides
now
the coat of glaze.
The wide Chinese brush
sweeps on
black, ochre,
cobalt, rust.

To the kiln,
and again the fire.
The colours,
iridescent,
glow and shimmer
and in the end,
no longer mutable,
cool and set.

Bone and breath
turned back to clay

morning light,
the sixth day.

Hands

My lover
had his hands frostbitten
in the north once,
and now the ends of his fingers
are numb,

causing him to sense
with the delicate inner flesh
of the fingers.

I watch how he smokes,
or picks up a cup,
the careful stroking way
he turns the pages
of a book,

remembering

the touch of his hands
on my breasts.

Chinese Puzzle

You say they've been civilized
longer than anyone, and this museum
proves it, with artifacts made
thousands of years before Christ:
implements, weapons, remnants
of that famous potentate in Sian
who loved his warriors into clay . . .

Consider the intricate carving
on this bronze sword, the iris blue
of porcelain, red cloisonné peonies
growing on the mirror of a palace
concubine. What is the link
between art and cruelty? Here
are the makings of war, slavery,
and notions of beauty that crushed

girls' feet into pairs of dead lilies.
See how exquisite the small shoes.
Like you, I could rave about loveliness
but instead I ask myself where
goodness and justice fit in. You'd
touch a finger to my mouth and chide,
Don't ask. Let civilization
make beauty without judgment . . .

Take this scroll, for example,
with cragged mountains, lone monk
by a cave. Observe the wet pines,
raven in mist, waterfalls lighting
the monk's smile. A courtier
imagined this wilderness among
tassels and brocade. Did either
painter or painted hear the muffled
weeping in the narrow passageways
that twisted into the city's heart?

In a Far City

Sampans toss and groan under our hotel window.
At two a.m. my daughter and I cannot sleep
together in this bed so many worlds
from home: our snow-hushed rooms, warm
and separate, changed to this stiff
intimacy under silk. Neither of us knows
the other's skin. Hers is smooth, blue as milk;
mine crinkled, scalded cream. We try

not to cough or sway the ancient mattress.
But I want to tell her how this dark
hotel's a buried city of women like us.
In this room we meet and part from our
mothers, children, lovers, breath.
This bed swings like a bridge
over all that divides us.

Ernest J. Berry

Three Haiku

power outage
the outside dark
lighter

long easter service
stained glass saints
cross the altar cloth

water spider
the spring sun
goes straight through

Have I Written to You

Across the wet
walkway in pink
vulnerability, earthworms —
driven up from
their world of soaked
tunnels.

At night
plants are breathing
with us, for us;
respiration, transpiration.

I want to say
incandescent,
phosphorescent
but
they seem to absorb light,
black holes
shadows of their day-selves.

Have I written to you
of the man
in this neighbourhood
who sings opera
each night about ten,
or rather, of his voice,
which travels to my window.

Those arias on the air
remind me again of
breathing.   Obscured by
trees, I don't know where he
sings — from window or porch, or
standing in a garden,
know only that his song
mingles with the exhalation
of greenery, pulling me
like light.

A Paris Blackbird

Along the Seine's left bank, near the Pont-Neuf,
on the mansard roof of my hotel, a scruffy blackbird
squats by a chimney pot. Every day for a week now,
I have listened to him sing his April *a cappella*.

Not once has he repeated the same song, not once
has he left for the chestnut trees by the river,
where he would have a better chance of being heard,
a better chance of enchanting some bronze-breasted female,

or lovers taking time off from noise. His song
is all that counts. It soars over terra-cotta chimneys,
its trills hushed by taxis, cars and trucks
coughing through the perpetual Parisian rush.

On the right bank of the Seine, three hours
into Le Louvre's maze, past Persian mosaics, glass-caged coins
and Egyptian amulets, I slip out of the tourist herd
and head for a chair in a corner of the Greek Hall.

I sit there, shoeless, numb with knowledge and history,
stare at the bust of an old woman,
                    labeled *Anonymous, Greek, 11 BC.*
She looks at me: weary, terrible with banality, lips open,
neck taut as if she were about to sing.

And as the crowds flock toward the Venus de Milo,
nod at her beauty, gawk at her perfect breasts, I look
at this nameless woman — as I did the scruffy blackbird —
and listen for the cry caught in her bronze throat.

English Flavors

   I love to lick English the way I licked the hard
round licorice sticks the Belgian nuns gave me for six
good conduct points on Sundays after mass.

   Love it when 'plethora,' 'indolence,' 'damask,'
or my new word: 'lasciviousness,' stain my tongue,
thicken my saliva, sweet as those sticks — black

   and slick with every lick it took to make daggers
out of them: sticky spikes I brandished straight up
to the ebony crucifix in the dorm, with the pride

   of a child more often punished than praised.
'Amuck,' 'awkward,' or 'knuckles,' have jaw-
breaker flavors; there's honey in 'hunter's moon,'

   hot pepper in 'hunk,' and 'mellifluous' has
aromas of almonds and milk. Those tastes of recompense
still bitter-sweet today as I roll, bend and shape

   English in my mouth, repeating its syllables
like acts of contrition, then sticking out my new tongue —
flavored and sharp — to the ambiguities of meaning.

August

We are alone again,
 children and friends have come
  and gone, a hush of sage

wafts through the air,
 I sew a button to your shirt,
  it's August — placid, fair.

You're writing in your room,
 looking up now and then
  to stare at the nasturtium

and lavender I planted by the gate,
 for their gold and purple thrusts,
  their sedulous reaching,

and when I bring your old
 frayed shirt to my lips,
  cutting the thread with my teeth,

I hold it there simply
 because it is yours, and has
  our smell, familiar and common.

I press the denim against my face,
 tasting the air in it, the sun,
  and realize how light it is,

how easily it could slip
 out of my hands, out of the moment —
  how the smallest distraction,

the slightest inattention
 could leave me here alone,
  with nothing but my face in my hands.

The Feather at Breendonck

      I am praying again, God — pale God —
here, between white sky and snow, by the larch
I planted last spring, with one branch broken at the elbow.
I pick it up, wave winter away, I do things like that,
call the bluebirds back, throwing yarn and straw
in the meadow, and they do come, so terribly blue,
their strangled *teoo-teoo*

      echoing my prayer *Dieu, Dieu* —
the same *Dieu* who stained the feather I found
in the barbed fields of the Breendonck Concentration Camp
near Antwerp in 1952. My father tried to slap it
out of my hand: *It's filthy.* But I held on to it —
I knew it was an angel's. *They only killed
a few Jews here,* he said, *seven, eight hundred, maybe.*

      So I wave their angels away with my feather,
away from my father, away from the terribly blue skies
over the Breendonck Canal, where barges loaded bricks
for Antwerp, where my father loaded ships for Rotterdam,
Bremerhaven and Hamburg — as Antwerp grew,
and the port expanded, and his business
flourished, and all the while he kept repeating:

      That's all we needed: a good war . . .

Brian Burke

pocket knife

he pulls a knife from his pocket
pries the blade & pares the wire coating
cutting parallel from the plug

he exposes the burnished copper strands
he'll twist together

later he'll peel back the yellow callous
pruning beneath his blackened fingernails
so pulling from his pocket the plastic tape
an electrician uses he is cleansed

he wraps the wires he joined — one lone flaw
in the weave — his thumb
the spool that sets the freezing evening spinning

we'll watch the interlacing lights
along the eaves of snow
blink   blink colour   & burn

the train through the far northwest

the train through the far northwest
stops six times
                              approaching
                 two seasons of least heat
before
someone fills the fields with snow

In the Zapotec Ruins

When you are cracked open, dance.
Rumi

In the Zapotec ruins of Monte Alban
is an ancient hospital, its walls lined with
bas-reliefs — textbook cases on slabs of stone.

A hunchback, a mongoloid.
Pregnant women with complications —
"The Dancers", archaeologists called them.

How did they ignore the curlicues
of fallopian tubes that floated inside the women
like musical clefs of fretwork on a violin?

One woman squats as if her baby
might emerge like corn from the ochre soil.
Another waits out the centuries,

baby's legs dangling between hers.
Doctors perform Caesarians while
ancient stone screams, hushed hands flutter.

In the dusty square, atrophied seed pods
of the jacaranda gape like silent castanets
among the lush violet blooms.

The Slave

from a painting

In the crowded market they arouse no interest:
four tall men in long robes doing business.
They surround a young Venus —
tiny peach breasts, pubic fuzz barely visible.
She is tethered by a bearded African
who looms behind, clutching her robe to his chest.
In the background, a limp dog lies belly-up.

The Arab buyer weighs her merits. Is she docile?
Will she breed well? Does she bear any scars?
He disguises his eagerness. She is a virgin,
and the asking price is high.

He wears a *burqa*; only eyes and nose visible,
and a large hand that pries apart the girl's lips,
explores her teeth, her tongue as if she were horseflesh.
She opens wide, allows the probing —
despite herself, lubricates the elegant fingers.

I do not see her shudder,
as a horse would with rippling withers.
She looks at him wide-eyed, her hip thrust out
provocatively, as if inviting him
to fondle her taut nipples, to slide
his long fingers slowly, slowly down her thighs
to the soft mound, to waken her
in the market place while all the men are watching.

Calling Out the Beautiful Names

From small towns   workers
who have never heard the word
radioactivity   farmers   miners
are conscripted for 180 days
assigned to *clean up the countryside*
make radiation maps   purple
for high levels. These maps
marking a landscape wounded
by wind   a mauve shadow settling
over fields and dairy farms   over
the lone dog's howl.

Liquidators. Beneath protective suits
their sweat runs in rivulets down
the wide arc of shoulder
and armpit. This meager covering
soon discarded   empty corn husks
trailing silk. Masks follow.
Death heads grimace in weeds.

No geiger counters here
no iodine to protect thyroids
blood tests stop
to stop the panic.

Some men *clean the power plant*
name the roofs over the reactors.
They call out the beautiful names
the beautiful names of women

Lyena
      Natasha
           Katya
                Marsha
                    Anna

Marsha is the fourth one
the mad one
cut open like a wound.

And the workers are sent
to the fields   to make radiation
maps   purple for high levels.
At night the men scrub their skin
in makeshift showers   remember
the taste of vodka. In amethyst dreams
they call out the names of women

Lyena
        Natasha
                Katya
                        Marsha
                                Anna

Belarus

Old women sit on a wooden bench
their mouths rounded
in the soft syllables of caring.

They remember the *banya*
heat rising from water over stones
the preparation of birch twigs

(picked in the third week of July)
for switches to soothe hard flesh.
Shawls and skirts ready for removal.

They speak of dead husbands
the greying beards they used to cut
black suits mended for church

and *bayans* filling their village
with accordioned language
folk songs rising in air.

But now the children   meek-eyed
and ill   some with scar tissue
from ear to ear

the familiar sign
of thyroid surgery
a necklace that contains no jewel.

And preserves from the garden
tomatoes and pickles bound in jars
passing on the particulars of death

how in autumn
they would rake leaves
gather them in for winter

fueling fires barely started
embroidering the threatened reaches
of wilderness. Stitches unravelling.

Marilyn Cay

heavy old red Buick and K.T. Oslin and I

clear, crisp autumn morning, crops
hanging, heads heavy, still
green-tinged, frost staying away
a fine day, heavy old red Buick
and K.T. Oslin and I
head down the field road, K.T. singing
as loud as I want, her voice
swelling out across pale barley tops
we stop on the sunken path, wheat
on both sides, tall rattling ripeness
beautiful, my heart is full
                K.T. calls
        across the broad expanse
            calls and calls, but
                no one comes

and K.T. and old red Buick and I
finally start out slow and head south
to alfalfa-wrapped hills, cropped closed
from dehy and we glide across the high ground
looking down on a farm
house and barns nestled
a mile and a half away
along the creek — six quarter-sections
the rectangle shape of my heart
we cross those hills, windows
down, hard edgy desperate music
resigned but rebellious, we reach
the approach to the road
hesitate for a moment before
pulling out between the two hills
head north along the west perimeter
of the *land*, pass under dark spruce, towering

➤

as generations pass beneath, Buick
turns east at the corner
almost on its own, like an old horse
who knows its way home
in a blinding storm, sometimes I think
it's worth whatever it costs to be here

Full Circle

(following Nurse's instructions)

Saturday afternoon: unfamiliar, this week
breaks routine, replaces shops
with standing by your narrow bed
as breathing ebbs. And I must strip
the rings from hands that cradled me.

I take three square-cut diamonds
on the band that bound
your wedding day to mine; the ring I wore
for 'something old' has blessed us both.

The others do not yield so easily. Flaccid fingers
mould around them. I have to edge
the next ring past your knuckle —
diamonds forever, fleeting their part
through your eternity.

I recall you laughing, explaining Grandma
picked your wedding ring — now finger-fixed
for fifty years. Its joy dissolved
when you were widowed, desiccated
without your life's leaven.

I dribble liquid soap around the gold
whose rubies gleam four decades,
soothe it off; catch, too, sapphires,
the substitutes you chose when those Dad bought
were stolen. Their memories weigh more
than stone.

I remember how you gave up hope
the day they handed you his wedding ring.
Today your rings burn brands into my palm.
I slip their burden on my fingers,
assume your place — and feel the circle close.

Denise Coney

Haiku

leaves turning —
   the grocer's change
   cool in my hand

Elegy

All of a sudden his darkened tone
passes through me with the
flowing breeze

He was twenty-nine
a produce clerk in charge of
rows & rows
of apples   bananas
& boxes of cherries
an orphan
who sang the blues
at a local café
after arranging fruit
all day

Singing the blues
his slant cap
shadowing his face
his steel guitar
held close for warmth —
strings stretched taut
while he belts out
I'm goin' to Louisiana
& plays his harmonica
& stomps his foot
the fragility of his face
at odds with his strong
lank body

I'm goin' to Louisiana
he sings   with incredible longing —
a single green light
on his sound board
does he see it —

➤

with those wolves
scratching at his door?
he finally decides
he's going to shoot that other man
the man in the mirror —
his face in irrevocable shadow

In the evening he plays
blues riffs like love's rhythms —
steel guitar & harmonica
keeping him afloat

In the morning he'll take
two drags and stay high
all day long piling oranges
apples & bananas

Is it too cliché to say that one
fine day it all falls down —
both men stopped flat & he hardly
knew them — only the howling
orphan at a pitch too high
for human hearing

And then pallbearers
carried him home
to blues heaven
at age twenty-nine

Epithalamion

She is smoking and talking with me
long after her lunch has been served.
"Eat. We have to eat," I say.

She agrees. What's really gnawing
is the recently vacant apartment downstairs.
The new tenants are anticipated like late night knocks

at the door, or a fire alarm,
they begin to embody a face-to-face struggle.
I say, "Tell them your music and singing,

and the way you break into dance
like you are taking off, like a bird flies,
is the way we all do it here." I refrain

from mentioning the killing heat,
the thunder crack across the air, the sudden wall of rain
closing off the constant sun.

She is intrigued by my intimacy.
She reminds me as I leave of solace, how she loves
the word. Solace, Joplin's Mexican Serenade,

his exquisite lyric rag, an epithalamion
for the second marriage, an evening lullaby,
sainted Louis Chauvin in the shadow,

a hand passing over your brow, a kiss on your shoulder
as we sit on these black iron steps
leading away from Holden Street not West Forty-seventh
and the breeze pushes up through the ventilated floor.

I am standing now, the next day, looking at the storm.
My light separated over years into bands of color. Now
on the Boulevard, one hour into the rain
the light is breaking through again.

Salt of the Earth

we are separated by a line drawn in chalk

The caption for a photograph from a far continent
persuades: Not forced laborers but Somalis working
in the salt mines. So much in our understanding
depends on the wood wheelbarrow posed on the beach.
So much is shown in their penetrating smiles.
In the end do we recognize the conscription of this labor?

Closer to home, in our own backyard,
the big dog stood on his hind legs and howled.
Who could not have heard? Let us not mistake
acknowledgement for comprehension. I will be clear:
    even enlightened, the bosses don't mean
    what we mean,
    when they say the same words.

Some time ago:
    Jeff was a journeyman carpenter out of work,
when he saddled up his motorcycle and made Denver
in under 30 hours. The boys who called him there
were spraying new construction, ceilings and walls,
inside white. They would divide up the subcontract dollars
at the end of the job-week,
wash their whistles down with Dr. Pepper,
rise to the hot morning fresh.
    He was ready and knew how to work.

Kathy followed in the VW
maybe a month later with a canary
riding shotgun. The bird expired
on the hundred-degree plain between Salinas and
the Colorado line. So much was broken
in the emigration
we could hardly count the loss.

What's done is done but today
the brotherhood showed us victorious and proud.
Sing that song about the open highway and that land
that's held at once by men and women standing together.

A Short History of Bio-Mechanics

We were sitting on our haunches in the Delta
packing wheel bearings, "Just glorified
parts changers!" like a sound from the other side
of a wall, sun danced in the darkness, olive on sand.
That was only thirty years ago. He had been
a mechanic in the real world. Deserved the big shop.
Is it not ironic that the beauty of the spoken word
is transparency, clear coat over candy apple shell?
What lets it through.

Going back against the grain this guy at work last week
was giving his impromptu history class on the subject:
How we had to go over there and show them how
to build some parts that would fit together.
Why, you couldn't take a wing from one plane
and expect it would fit another. When this
might have been is anybody's guess, but time was
if your Rolls radiator needed fixed, you sent it back
to the machinist who signed it. A little story:
Rolls caught wind that the Brough Superior
was advertised as the Rolls-Royce of motorcycles.
The foreman dressed everyone in white coats,
white gloves, and set about fitting the best parts
from the shelf into one machine. Timed perfectly,
the Rolls inspectors saw what they were led to see.

Today, when I want a genuine GM part
I'm not always particular where Beacon Auto
or PEP boys get it. But I might look for that signature.
I might not trust the long nomenclature of the part
number, the sequence of digits that's so military,
it's little use to my Chevrolet. I might want to look
for a signature, the one always called the Union Label.

Terrance Cox

The Devil's Music

Take, for telling instance, case of Georgia Tom:

he, a blues pianist, early '20s, who
tours TOBA, tents & Jim Crow halls
as professor in Ma Rainey's band
vamps hot stuff to her black bottom:
show-biz, sin & misery, irony & liquor —

ostinato, standard changes

On in raucous '20s later, Georgia Tom
company of Tampa Red, guitarist
reaches, by Illinois Central, epicentre
in Chicago by ten inch dozens
puts out hokum most salacious:
house-rent jams, ribaldry up-tempo —

ostinato, standard changes

Devil had Georgia Tom but good
until, off on road to Damascus date
year of our Lord 1930
snap, like that, seized by holy spirit
Georgia Tom, saved, takes sacred vow
to play no more wicked music:

becomes that Thomas A. Dorsey who
invents modern gospel, composes
'Precious Lord', 'Peace in the Valley'
'My Desire' & three hundred other
'songs of praise' for Jesus

Stalwart, forty righteous years, he weaves
barrelhouse, jump & gin-mill jazz
into holy cloth, comps for & conducts
southside choir, Pilgrim Baptist, sanctified —

ostinato, standard changes

Photo-Documents 1940:
Fighter Pilots Resting on Alert

Too fledgling to take to air —
barely out of teens — perhaps not that . . .

Muffled in sheepskin
tousled heads resting on folded arms.
Stripped of bravado
their vulnerability exposed in sleep.

Soon to kill dispassionately, or
fall as Icarus, wings melted
on a funeral pyre;

these boys, not yet men
who shoulder death on silver wings;
perhaps remembering in their dreams
those they've left behind
before madness takes their breath away.

Sandra Dempsey

Belles of Autumn

outside my window
a little breath
of wind and a
hundred thousand
brittle autumn leaves
tumble from their
branches and
onto the hordes
of fallen comrades
below
the muffled clattering
sound is as if
God had wrapped
warm hands
around their bells

Ernest Dewhurst

Storm Lamp

A glazed eye saw me home
from school on winter days.
The lantern in the lane
would nerve me through
the shadows to the farm.
Glass-cased and paraffin-fed
(my Holy Spirit light)
the pale flame signalled
passport through a goblin gloom.
Defied wind, hail and rain.
Gave reassuring winks
on windier days.

Posted like a dog to chase
a boy's imagined fears
the storm lamp never closed
its eye on me. My father
timed it to my bus. Next
to a dog the lamplight
was his closest evening aide.
He swung the lantern
on his nightly rounds
to close the poultry sheds
against the fox. Hooked
on a nail, it cast his hands
across a ghostly labour ward,
a farrowing sow. Held high,
it lit his late night check
on sickly cow. For all of us
it gleamed our cobbled way
to closets down the yard.

When power sneaked up the hill
we steeped ourselves
in farmhouse watts. Threw out
the lamps which strained
our eyes. But out of doors
the storm lamp lingered on
and may be flickering still
in some outlandish place.
Spirit-powered and lifting
some boy's spirits now.

Summer in Southern Germany, 1995

I   High Wind in Augsburg

There's a storm cranking up over Haunstetten.
The wind wheels through these rooms,
urgent, fresh from the woods
where it scattered swans
over green lake
from a querulous sleep.

Siemens' vast lot is nearly empty,
a few cars huddle against the wind,
desolate, their owners lost.
It is 5 a.m., and a grey light
seeps from the sky, clouds move
with deliberate speed toward me, birds shriek.

It is the same storm that followed us home
                            from Munich last night,
the same wind sweeping the *Englischer Garten* and Dachau.

II Augsburg on a Clear Day

You can see the Alps from here, they say,
on a clear day, standing on the edge
of the dammed-up Lech.

A haze of damp heat, like Bangladesh,
sun beating down on my head and back,
flat fields unfold on either side,

dotted with *Dörfer* — neat white houses
with slanted orange tile roofs,
flower boxes at each window, hot pink, mauve.

But always, in the not-too-distant east,
a shadow streaming to the sky, like smoke.

III Dachau

These walls are clean,
neat cots stand in stacked rows.
Between the barracks
two lines of poplars gleam.

Barbed wire coils
across the ditch,
above the fence —
watchtowers mute in the sun.

Dazzled by light,
my eyes blink:
pebbles rise from the ground
like ghosts.

We drag our feet
across the past.

Gerald England

St. Ninian's Cave

Past giant rhubarb and bluebell banks
the path stepstones the stream

March marigolds grow
beneath tall, fungi-clad trees

Beyond the pebble-strewn beach
the cave penetrates the cliff

From ledges of sea-thrift
water drips over the entrance

Up the multi-creviced rock
a spider climbs

My son lifts a placed pebble
to find a shiny tiny five-pence piece

The dog sniffs seaweed entangled
in the flotsam of a consumer age

St. Ninian does not hide here now

Over in Whithorn they exhume his age
and parade it for the paying public

Janice Faria

Lace

How many times during that winter
did I rise early, dress in the darkness
and hurry out into the gray stillness,
past the small houses, kitchen lights on,
narrow chimneys releasing the first
slim streams of smoke.

At the church door, always the same
rush of warmth; candles, incense
and Latin words. Kneeling at the marble
rail, hands beneath the starched white cloth,
feeling a Presence move within, sure,
like a child moving in the womb.

That time of certainty, flawless
like the lace edge of the cloth
intricate and enduring. That was
before I understood the delicacy
of lace, how easily it becomes undone.
Once snagged, how difficult to repair.
Once unravelled, how impossible to replace.

Penny L. Ferguson

Legacy Of Shadows

I

In October drizzle we drift
over the graveyard —
my husband, further along with the car;
my aunt, a distance to the left;
and my young son tripping behind me
on the narrow paths at the feet of graves.
My aunt's search for you has led us
to Mount Ollivet Cemetery.
Amid crumbling headstones
we look for your name "Catherine Sampson."
Your presence being narrowed to this place,
we hope to narrow it further.

I skirt austere stones —
mementos of faces vaguely remembered
in faded family photos —
looking for a simple marker,
your poverty felt even here
these seventy years later.
The Cemetery Commission says you are
in this field sown with despair
but they cannot say where —
perhaps in an unmarked or mass grave.
There would have been no opulence
for a turned away girl dying of tuberculosis
in the service of the convent.
Did nuns come to stand moist-eyed over your grave
mourning your passing
or did a lone priest, robes whipping in the wind,
motion you toward God?

56

A writer, I could create for you a history,
but it could not be more tragic
than the legacy of shadows
that has drawn us to this place.

II

Your mother died and father quickly remarried;
step-mother drove you out to work;
raped by the man you served;
sent home heavy with child;
scorned; delivered of child
and sent forth again to another man —
another violation; branded a "whore"
as your belly grew large and shamed them;
untimely ripped from your babies
and sent to Halifax to serve
brothers and sisters whose goodness,
like coals, seared your soul.

In October drizzle we search for you —
my aunt — your granddaughter;
I — your great-granddaughter;
my son — your great-great-grandson.
Though your home and children were taken from you,
you have not lost your family.
We have searched and come to grieve your life and pass-
ing,
to tell you your legacy of shadows
has found a place of light in our family heart.

Rina Ferrarelli

The Streetcar

Across the trestle at night
an island on wheels
a floating village
a picture gallery
each brightly-lit frame
a portrait
        of people
together by chance

The Bricklayers

repaving the street near my house
talk Italian as they work,
a southern dialect.
They're Abbruzzesi
descendants of an ancient people
who made roads and aqueducts
for the Romans, and paths
that others would follow.
"I was a stone mason back home,"
the boss tells me, and I know
that like my mother's father,
he built houses for a living.
He gives orders in Italian
and a young man answers in English.
They're fathers and sons,
in-laws and *paesani.*
In the space they've opened between the curbs
they measure carefully
from the middle to the edge,
from the edge to the middle,
matching new bricks with the old,
blending the colors to look good.

Afterlives

We took up the carpet, laid bare
the maple floor, the long and short strips
side by side, end to end,
fine-grained heartwood, several shades
of blond, of brown, and a variety of figures,
streaks and waves hidden for years
under wall-to-wall grey-lavender wool,
to protect it from damage,
from the children's play and curiosity,
their clumsiness, but also
our careless rushing, those years
a stream at flood, heads barely above water,
fingers clutching the rim of something
we couldn't even see in the churning water,
the dimness. And now this calm,
this flecked expanse, as beautiful
as when we first moved in,
a revelation that it could keep like this
under the rug, the layers of dirt,
the pounding of feet, the furniture
dragged from end to end, that only a little work
could make it glow as if amber, released,
had spread over the surface.
It's too late now for many things,
but how great to uncover, discover again under us
something solid, vulnerable, and joined to last.
Bare feet touching bare wood, I grasp
at this afterlife, this straw-colored joy.

Fat Woman Dancing

Owed to MLI

Last night the janitor
Looked down across the office atrium
To the one dimly lit window
And glimpsed a fat woman dancing
Amongst the chairs and desks
Of an office made suddenly bigger
By its inability to confine
Her arms and legs all akimbo.

She saw him watching her,
Which only increased her insistence
On joy.

Janet Fraser

Conrad Black and Me

an unemployed worker's dream
tonight Conrad Black appears
six inches away from me
in a stiff pin-striped suit
a small smile creases his gleaming face
his sleek boar's body
looks ironed, or flattened by a girdle
i tell him i need a job
couldn't he snap 1 more unit
into place on the smooth rolls
that move his newsprint around the *Globe?*
and i continue, wheedling
with whatever girl power i own
hips grinding, eyes softening
but the flicker in his gray eyes
dies, the smile withers and
waking i remember
i'm a 41-year-old wife
with a lumpy body
and a Wal-Mart Canada wardrobe
my cup's coffee flowing over
the Classifieds

Michael Fraser

The Course of Miracles

wind slithers
past erect gophers

paper tumbles down
grinds its feather weight along
my leg
      scrapes
            the bare ground

thunderheads curve eastward
                  throughout
                    the bending shale

armfuls of rain

Elizabeth Gourlay

Roses Have Names

They are soon gone, the roses
        White Wings,
        Perle d'Or,
        pink Baby Face

all petals dropped from
        striped Perfecta
        Dortmund
        Duval
        French (my favourite) Lace

leaves draggle from
        Compassion
        Honor

limbs, bare, do not evoke the Prima's dance . . .

November now and time to
        put away the hoe, the sprayer
        protect, with earth,
        the tender crowns from frost

        already we have mounded
        Chaucer
        Ellen
        and the robust Wife of Bath

November now   I walk a stony path
        past
        Promise
        Love
        and New Year
        I walk, my fingers crossed —

Rawsilk

I want to be bedraggled in rawsilk

I want to be bedraggled
in rawsilk in the early morning

I want to be bedraggled by the rawsilk of your skin
that keeps me awake until early morning

Cargo

For Lou

What was chained below was not as precious as
What the slaves carried within.
It bound them more securely than the
Vast water that separated them from their land;
It would tell how intangibles of the heart
Could purchase and possess evil, death.

Some bodies rebelled
Soon sensing this journey of so-long-a-time meant no return —
Death restored their ascendancy.
Those surviving the crossing, the lacking,
Never owning justice, and dying always,
Must have 'visioned their daily grief become our ever comfort,
Must have hoped so strong desire became fact.

Generations untold of that wretched voyage, lost land,
Constant struggle, now know often
The same blood clots in slave and master.
Both accomplish a communion of grief and gain.
Precious jewels — crystalline —
Forged above deck in sun, salt, sea.
Below, pressured in darkness, lack and death:
Diamonds.

Steel Man

Open Hearth heat
5 metal doors rise and fall in turn
dust-covered shovels and men
like a Gatling gun circle and fire
dolomite with accuracy and precision

Tapping out
long bar down the oven's throat
First Helper and 4 men raising the rod
hammering the clay plug to release
liquid metal to race down
clay-lined runner into a gaping ladle

Finishing the melt
thick wool coats behind the furnace
fiery stream seeks the ladle
quickly a shovel of moly
a few sticks of mag
like a pinch of salt
to finish the recipe
the full bucket inches carefully
from the floor of the pit
6 fearless knights in wool armor and helmet
fling 50 pound bags of coke
a crusty heat seal
glowing tower of sparks signals
making steel

A Touch of Northern Ireland

Growing up in the south, I have an automatic
reflex to "northern" anything, much less
the northern half of a country. Take
Vietnam or Korea for recent examples.

While roaming through the Republic of Ireland,
we neared a town with the foreboding name
of Enniskillen. We touched the North.

In the highway, blocking our lane, a wall.
An impersonal traffic light signalled
when to go around the offset blockade.

Through the brief maze and a young man
stops us. Red hair, freckles, very young.
Also uniformed, with an automatic weapon,
and no smile. "Why are you here?"

Tourists. Stammering. Neck hair bristles.
"Open the boot." Nothing to hide.
Zigzag through the second maze. We drive.
We stop. We face each other. No smiles.

The Collector

Sourwood dangles
orange seeds
from barest branch
as if to tempt
her gaze away
from heather's yield
of blossoms white
as starlight.
Rooted in rocks
atop the ridge
Sawbriar leans
green and slick
across the trail,
tears hikers' flesh,
licks its thorns
along a line
of blood.
Where rivers once
pushed mountains up
November strolls,
shaking black pods
of coins
and with much ease
plucks each tree.
How the leaves tremble
like old men's hands
in wind
reaching for fire.

The Cancer Came

queer chill
locks onto
the pounding squeeze
each panicked thought
multiplies

blood pulses
into each vein
a stampede of devils
inside the brain
blocks the light

the body rejects
the will
a surrender to help
helpless in surrender
denial finally fails

the heart in rhythm —
one deep breath
one shallow
the last like mist
a pale echo over water

Earl Keener

Right Field Lines

I was sitting on a spike keg watching the game.
We'd been working on the tracks that run behind
the field. It resembled a pinball machine —
the ball bouncing off awakening pegs — I got it!
I got it! And no one had. A train arrived
from the east, its engine a needle pulling
blue thread. I watched the center fielder chase
a line drive, veering with a mind of its own
towards a stand of sassafras. The game was lost
in a shuffle of ore hoppers closing like a zipper
on space. Sitting, I thought of my dad
pulling a zipper on a leather pouch,
a cumulus of pipe smoke above his head.
I thought of my mother, sewing a button
on a striped shirt, and of Jerry —
living further away than miles can measure.
I felt whatever passed in life was not gone
but tucked away in a place beyond losing.
I remembered standing, just so, dreaming
down the right field line — a ball speeding at me
so fast I could hardly react. I sat until light
flickered between cars like footage
at the end of a film. The caboose was a blue punctuation.
A brakeman stood near the diamond
waiting to throw a switch. His face was deep wrinkled.
His eyes sparkled like the bits of mica
in the ballast between ties, sparkled like my mother's needle.
I looked toward the game. The home team was in the field
and a translucent thread was lifting on the wind
as if someone were knitting the sky.

Wallflower

The crew is high and giggly
so I'm off in a clump of weeds
looking for a katydid.
All evening I've made noises
like a damaged clarinet.
Six stacks rise above
the mold yard like flutes
without stops. The sinter plant
scrubber is a tuning fork
sustained to madness.
Once I stood on a narrow plank,
too high inside a boiler,
a lost automaton in a giant
pipe organ — my foreman's face
a mask in the hatchway behind.
Now I am a gandy dancer.
Morning glories trumpet
over the pox-faced slag;
punk-haired thistles bob in the flood
lights. A coke engine's wailing
down a fret-board track.

Larry Kimmel

Taking Notice After a Long Dark Night

The dew is not yet burned
from the orchard grass —

Crows range the open sky
on easy wings —

To the north,
a chain saw pitch-shifting
gnars a tune —

The forsythia is yellow, the lawn
salt-crusted with Spring Beauties —

A wasp dangles by —

To the north,
a great conifer falls, sputtering
like firecrackers —

Raising the mug I hold, I taste
my morning coffee —

How clear, how crisp the air!

Philomene Kocher

Two Haiku

rosehips and roses
and buds all on the same bush
August evening

all handshake
farmer eloquence:
I miss him too

Ken Kowal

song of the butcher

so honest a repetition
in the habit of his life
ending & beginning
days with the faithful
ritual of sleep
each day a passage
through an uncertain
monotony of calendars
within a solitude
of customers

he demanded sharpness
of his tools, strength
from his hands
gloved with blood
delicate bone dust

he severed flesh from
hard bone & pale fat
tossed thin slivers
into a blood-teared bucket

he displayed his chops
fanned on a tray like
a winning poker hand

he scraped fat off the block
with a coarse wire brush
scarred a hollow cross-hatch
each day deeper into the grain
while the four corners rose up
like the horns of a beast

i dream my father's hands

i dream my
father's hands
jig the rod
back & forth

Rover circles
groans & settles
down to sleep

the black Mercury
chugs rings of smoke
returns a thin arc
of water to the lake

behind our boat
the wake spreads out
like two hands
unfolding a letter

rod bends
his grip tightens
as a smallmouth
rainbows a spray
of droplets
into air

my

eyes open
returning with
the sense of
how the dead
in need
call out

one's name

Joan Latchford

Armistice, East Dean, 1932

Soft November morning
frost-melt glints on drab grasses and
a child's gumboots scramble
after the gardener's even plod . . .

past the kitchen garden
smelling of cabbages
the finger-chilling Brussels sprouts still
stand to attention . . .

up the breathless hill to the bantam run
and the little cock's shrill crow
(King George likes *two* bantam eggs
for his breakfast) . . .

the handle of the chicken pail
winces back and forth, then
clanks to the ground at the boom of the big guns
sounding across the downs . . .

"What is it, what is it?" I whisper
watching him stand straight
as the Brussels sprouts until the reverberations
die away on the moist air . . .

He wears wire thin gold rings in his ears
"for his eyes"; their gaze fixed
to an interior distance of mythic conflict
he names to me as "the Great War."

John B. Lee

Sinkers

for two boys drowned in Port Stanley, June 1998

The lake leapt up at the end of the pier
and licked him from his feet
like the sticky tongue
of a huge insatiable beast
and he was nearly seventeen
and stupid to the storm
which was ravenous
and rolled him of his soul
loud as stone rumble
his body tumbling in the underwash
the skein of his bone
lathing out
a crone slubber of dead wool
unwound from the sheep foam of his last breathing
wild weather
sumping the pier-hollows
where on better days
boys had sat on the roof slope
of concrete
casting in the calm
where their hooks plooped
like the final fatal skip a pebble takes
before it drops in the deep
where fish live
and the lines hung
like drowned marionettes dancing
a dance of veils
where the green gods
wave their weedy hair
and think.

And his friend saw him go
and leapt in after
where the blind wash swilled
and he was the second lad lost
that day
as the hero chases the fool
while boats bumped together
jumping on their harbour ropes
and wise captains watched the rough rain
rising backwards
where the breakers slapped their tails
these two doomed boys entered a second illusion
while coffin makers hammered cold homes.

Perhaps the younger boy
had stood bubbling baby talk
in the yo-yo of his mother's harness years before
perhaps he'd lain
in his father's open arms
mocking love by lolling there
perhaps he'd dangled his legs
into the danger beyond his bed
where the water-bright linoleum
of his own blue room
swallowed life.
Perhaps he'd awoken that very day
planning the evening
and the day after
regarding the dog-eared calendar
to measure the lapse till summer

➤

and as I remember
riding the bus to the Rodney pool
as a boy
and being called *sinker*
by the girls
while we splashed
in the cold shallows
like minnow tubs full of silver sunlit fins
and then stood shivering on the deck
in the skinny shock of wet light and July breathing
we were pale
and didn't think of dying
our arms out and stiff
as laundry starched by summer
and I became *tadpole*
the second season
following the guide rope
out where my feet slipped
and caught the weird half-gravity
of water
while those life guards
shrilled their whistles
like cruel birds

and I thought of the boy
I was, watching the lake
later, seeing Erieau
seeing Port Stanley, seeing Dover
seeing Dicky Lowell's drowned father
pulled fat as a fish
from his first grave
and I see those two boys
suddenly disappearing from the end of the pier
battered lifeless
and dumb as waterlogged wood
their deaths sinking
in the wintering hearts of their fathers
like the long cold adrenal needle
of a gorgon's gaze.

The Woman with
the Hem of Her Coat Hanging

With the hem of her coat hanging
the woman is walking home from the village
after the rain the crooked river of her stockings
follows a vein to the heart.
She carries groceries
for her husband
and her heels hammer
the gravel
with a purpose of miles
like a child learning to build
on the rounded shoulders
of the road.
Hers, ditch music
blue chicory and wild carrot
corn stalks
wealthy green dancers
in a soft-whispered waltz of summer wind
the wheat field's golden worry
and the boys hoe dogbane
from beans in the heat
while she with her embrace of sugar
the small sweet child of the sack
asleep in her arms
with the deadweight drift of a dreaming daughter
and the broken stitch in the hem
makes her seem importantly poor
a small philosophy
of garment rather than want of style

she talks in silence
to the world of mending
our way
in the rather-this-than-that
of her choosing
not for the gossip of dogs between barns
nor the bull bellows
above the door below the mow
but she thinks with hands to the eggs still warm
like lights turned low in a room just left
and she muses on the seen darkness
the mother-safe hour
after understanding
when sureness deepens
and concern swings its precious circle
round a single house.

Influenza Epidemic, 1918

that year with October came a sickness
sorrowing with the great war
and all the sad performers
passed through pallor farm to farm
cold graces
and late griefs
a multitude among the quiet rooms
after the loss of loved sons
and the news that chalked across
the water shock by shock
to make a village list
a pewter scroll of church wall heroes
in the ill-coloured light
fevered on the maple pews
a shadow from the proper alphabet
of men too dead
to say, the tributary
veined off from the larger blood's blue wine
but all the ill
in that conceit of filthy weather
died, dithering off
with the loss of wives, sisters, daughters
husbands, cousins, brothers, sons
uncles, fathers, mothers and more
entering an ever evil loneliness
which consumed us helpless house by house
beneath the glassy racket of a sleety wind
until the fatal fever swept the field
and left a few untouched

the sunset like a swathe of lamb's blood
painted on a distant sky
and all the buried hope
came crocusing up
like eggshells emptied by the birth of birds
cruel April
fastened by a nail or two of rain
the sheep's hide of a cloudy month
show the clear blue art of Easter
and to learn the meaning
of life when our love laments
its lack of strength to bear our loss
to save us from the unspeakable dying of a child
when all the suffering stones
forget us
and no one weeps
to hear our names aloud.

Grandmother Sonnet

Last night the moon was pale as painted stone
And like the lime-washed granite of a barn.
A man might build this month and stand alone
Beneath the stars of heaven hard to learn.
Among the many milk ghosts of the mind
The ditch remembers what the field has known
Where water runs ahead and leaves behind
The silt that steals its meaning from the loam.

And if by strength of will the field comes clear
I think of work that carries off the land
Whereon the frost might heave another year.
There is a stronger heart, a stronger hand.
A sister to the moon; a smaller tide —
The shadow of the blood she feels inside.

I, Henry Tudor

At fifty-five, I am not kingly now.
I would you'd seen me in my younger days.
Eighteen I was, when I first wore the crown.
In archery and wrestling I excelled.
When I played tennis, all the ladies swooned.
As for the hunt, I never seemed to tire.

But I made time, too, for the gentle arts.
I sang and played the lyre. Soft now, don't smile;
for I was honest then. I did not lie
and had I not been born to take the throne
the need might not have risen;
for men lie most when they must govern states.

Still, lies aside, I knew my Scripture well;
Defensor Fidei for Pope Leo Tenth
— words placed upon the coinage of my realm.
That German upstart, Luther, called me names.
"King Heinz," he mocked. That didn't bother me.
"Lubberly ass," though, I could not forgive.

As to my wives, what can I say of them?
The first one, Katharine of Aragon,
was forced on me when my dear brother died
so her rich dowry'd not return to Spain.
Thus, I became, at the sweet age of twelve,
my brother's widow's keeper.

In fifteen twenty-five I wanted out.
She'd borne no son to carry on my name
and, with my golden beard and auburn hair,
ladies were soon attracted to my side.
I made the Church of England come to pass
so dark-eyed Anne Boleyn could be my bride.

➤

Anne's temper and demands soon wearied me.
I had her put to death, then wed her maid.
Jane gave her life in bearing me a son.
Alas, unlike Boleyn's Elizabeth,
Edward was sickly from the very start.
By now, I was a much-maligned monarch.

Plain Anne of Cleaves was never to my taste.
Thomas Cromwell engineered that union,
but I annulled it. She remained untouched.
I had Cromwell beheaded. That same day
I took fair Catherine Howard as my bride.
She proved untrue and lost her head as well.

They called me egotistical and vain.
It's true, I dominated Parliament
but under my strong hand
the land grew rich.
Those who opposed my ways, I laid to rest
without their heads.

Catherine Parr, my sixth wife — and my last
— may well survive me. I'm a broken man
— a mass of flesh, my ulcerous leg unhealed.
No doctor's skill can cure my syphilis.
But, ah, God's teeth! I would you'd seen me then
when I was young.

Tanis MacDonald

Phantom Limb

I

My uncle got his wooden leg in the war,
used to knock on it like it was a small door
that opened inwards, my uncle asking for
permission to enter himself. He claimed
the leg was hollow, and bet me a quarter
he'd eat more roast and Yorkshire pudding
at dinner. My mother told me not to stare,
but when he sank deep into a soft chair,
an inch of dark polished wood showed
between rolled pantcuff and sober black sock;
a firm branch, a solid weapon if brandished,
if swung. My uncle was a tall tree, a redwood
hoisting himself from the easy chair, stumping
down the hall to the dinner table. He never said
whether he woke at night to a burning itch,
the old leg calling him from the mud where
he had left it and another boy who screamed
for him and mother as the stretchers
bore him around a curve in the trench.

II

All the adults insisted she was fine,
adjusting so well to her prosthesis,
that lisping antiseptic word,
mashing together prophylactic and hypothesis,
sex and theory, a guess about desire.
When I sat on the empty space on her bed,
she said *Get off my leg*. Her replacement limb
stood false sentry in the hospital closet,
leaning against her pea jacket
like a tipsy sailor's mate, the molded foot
already sporting her worn loafer, the left one,
an impostor at the ball, Cinderella with a limp.

(At night, the leg hopped through the children's ward
like a pogo stick, practical as a nurse,
pausing by the sickest bed to draw the fever
off the child's skin, warming foam flesh
to real skin, Pinocchio's legacy,
this last belief in normal.) I hated
the songs at her funeral, and the way someone
pressed a packet of seeds into my hand, for
a hope garden. I ate them instead, ground them
between my teeth, savage. I went to
my dance class like it was any Wednesday,
my legs bowed and imperfect in the mirror,
chrysanthemum seeds rubbing the ridges
of my hard palate, bruising
every word.

Carol L. MacKay

Radium Dial

camel hair strands tickle her
with what she can buy
she pulls them through high centred lips
softening to a fine point

on the break they stage closet comedies
raised Marx brows   dip and float
into poltergeist goatees
tumbling beneath the cool swing of the bulb

she paints lightning bugs on her fingertips
they remind her, somehow, of the
Cottingly Fairies
almost hearing the hum of beating wings
in newspaper photographs

then, she's back in her lacquered desk
one of the painting ladies in a row
watching her face on the dial

     a meat market stood here
     before the fruit stand
     the Luminous Plant before
     the earth squealed
     they dug the girl up
     decades later, body encased in lead

     banged her down in the back
     of the Suburban, the driver noticed
     a hum
     down the highway.

Joy Hewitt Mann

My Mother Used to Be a Singer in a Band

I remember every word of songs
my mother used to sing.
She could stretch a smile to last a week
feeding us with her used-to-be's.
Used to be a singer in a band,
stiff-legged shifts from one to four,
waxing floors to make the dead ends meet,
nights in her eyes that made me blush —
she sweeps the tufts of red hair from her face
(bad dye job done for cheap)
her quiet voice rubbed raw with years
"Drinkin' rum and co-ca-co-la"
Johnny's puppy-bum wagging
Jessie's teetotum across the floor.

She likes the home (at least I think she does)
— she called me Madge the other day,
her dead sister's name.
Jessie talks of struggles in the West.
Johnny's faith hangs rabid on his face.
And Mother stares and smiles at walls.
We are the used-to-be's that fled her mind —
I remember every word of songs
my mother has forgotten now.

Horses to Ride

The farrier's son
loves the fleshy girl with garlic-breath
who laughs
"You'll break your neck"
as he swings from horse to horse
over the musky stalls
stroking flanks with eager thighs
thewy arms clutching crossbeams
while whinnies and prickly nickers
and steam rising in warm yeasty smells
to feed the air
seep through his skin
as he turns on love's great witless wheel
breaking his neck on the clapping of her hands
offering himself on a swarm of flies
lithe body gliding into gap-toothed smiles
and wide hips (and fat babies)
when the horses
are bedded down
when her laughter is put to sleep.

Grace Notes

I

you are my going to myself to gather
        myself
home

you are my home

2

how your vertebrae curve against mine
when we huddle in

arranging what we know
around what centre?

how we feel the workings
of each in each

the muscled speech
and slackening into sleep

3

if there is no spirit we can name
still, all our bright language will come back at us —
dew on our heads

if language is a construct, conduit,
what of that?

4

sometimes the companion is the beloved
and sometimes the beloved is a
kind of sharer of tasks

harnessed there,
you glance at each other
through blinders
remembered meadows

5

too often we are too tired, numb,
to turn to each other

almost lost, the desire
that otherwise might come flaring

6

there is always the possibility:
one of us lank-haired,
vomiting up sputum

one finding the pressure points
on the other's spine
willingly, willingly

one hooked up to tubes,
the other waiting
in a close room

➤

7

or I, holding your unmuscled flesh
guiding you toward the shower

o love, let us be true

all the pieces falling around us
and the cries of our unborn dreams

when you are old and grey and full of sleep

8

in your first vision of me
I floated toward you, veiled —
you naked as Adam

who will go first
all passions blown
still hungering

and who will linger,
o my second skin,
face within my face?

Bruce Meyer

At T.S. Eliot's Columbarium, East Coker

In my beginning is my end.
In my end is my beginning.

No mean little hole in the wall, but a place
fit for embarkation on a long cold journey
where the traveler returns with his face
altered by the highways and mountains
his soul has conquered, where the only trace
of the spirit is in the silence that strains
to rise above the weight of its own gravity.

Anything is capable of taking flight, even
the word for a niche where ashes are stored —
columbarium — speaks of wings spread and drawn,
beating thin air, a homing, a migration or return.
The lectern where the gospel nests, a golden
eagle in Victorian brass, cannot be ignored:
the verses hatch. What rhythms can we learn?

I was talking with the verger who pointed out
the granite plaque. His eyes were rheumily tired
like one who had cared too long and thought
too hard about the details of a little-visited
corner, a place tuck-pointed and neatly swept,
kept kempt for the faithful, the message revisited
like a text: *be patient until time has expired.*

➤

If you are going to believe in anything, then
choose to believe in poetry, a dimension where
time never treads, an eternal still of summers when
a rose never lost its perfect bloom and beauty
and truth walked as naked and free of sin
as Adam and Eve. If it sounds promising, there
is still room to imagine paradise and eternity.

And here, in the mossy scent of last Easter
and the solemn white lilies that became poetry,
perhaps time does move a slow pace faster
and the dead see beyond the end of temporality
where the great everlasting poetic Master
rhymes death with breath and life with strife
knowing in the end of ends there is only life.

Renee Norman

In Benign Remembrance

the sun
a medallion of light
in a mohair fog
warm on your feeble knees
fuzzy with the memory
of that jacaranda tree
on African soil
the day your husband died
miles away
and you felt free
the touch of young girls' hands
upon your own
a father's newsprint stamped forever
in your brain
a mother's poetic legacy
written over with a woman's lot

i lived with you three days
until you died
swirled like the fog
among the chapters of your life
wondered:
how did Gina die?
and what about your son, Peter
daughter, Marcia
as you sat in that nursing home
a grey fog
on your knees
in search of a sun
a drop of benign remembrance

the newspaper eulogized
a matriarch of poetry
equal in scope and talent
to an earl
the mother of us all
you were not about to go forgotten

this fog
the sun
your poems mist
on my cheeks
where your words burn now

Note: Dorothy Livesay died December 29, 1996,
as I was reading her memoirs.

H.F. Noyes

City Sequence

homeless beggar —
the itch of his clothes
all down my spine

subway poster —
I can touch the face
of the missing child

ripe night harvest —
rubbish pickers flock
with the early birds

deserted park —
chill winds arrow in
on the sunning vagrant

old bag lady
chooses her winter coat —
by the smell

R.U. Outavit

Don't Stand Too Close To The Mirror

My mother's hands are
what I remember most
folded neatly in the coffin
so still and peaceful
the dress sleeves carefully
arranged to conceal
the wrists
I use an electric shaver
but I don't care what brand
whatever I get for Christmas

Omaha Beach, 6th June 1944

Seasick and spilling the close stink of fear
Into a grey-brown dawn of sudden death
On T.V. the soldiers' flickering images clear
The troubled naval landing craft beneath
Malignant guns. Out of the swollen tide,
As heavy-packed with innocence as pride,
They disembarked that dreadful day
To face the rain of wet and German lead.
Nothing more real than the sudden way
On screen those lumps of men slumped dead —
Men of Utah, California, gold Virginia
Slain in their thousands in a foreign land —
Nothing more real save the feelings there are
For those who fought for freedom on that strand.

The White Table, 4 a.m.

You are asleep my hope-and-all
in the guest room above the night wind
while I, at the white table,
ponder nervous sounds of yet another night,
a wakeful speck of metropolitan thought.

It is the hour of the burglar
and the anxious father, of late lovers
and tragic drinkers — and we
who shuffle the endless pack of words
share the fever and fret of them all.

There is no silence outside the mind
but revealing noise: the bitty tick of clock
scratching the wall, the wailing
identity of police cars pursuing
their morality through suburban dreams,

and, if I listen hard enough,
beyond the screams of insecurity — no,
not the scrunching of death's heel
on gravel! — but something more: always
the murmur of impossible truth, blank
and white as this table on which I write.

Margaret Pain

Millerground, Windermere

The mists are down
on the mountains,
it is the time to look at ferns,
moss-covered boulders, trunks and logs,
hear the busy sucking
of water upon small stones,

explore outcrops
and the tiny expressions of lichens,
the innumerable varieties of grass,

and observe
the firm outspokenness
of foxglove
against cliffs and stone walls,
the experiments of roots,
and enjoy intimate vistas
of clefts.

Now is the time,
also,
to turn away
and let the
deep thought come,
entirely
by surprise.

Kathy Pearce-Lewis

For a Lost Miner

Drop now
to earth's hollow god
exploding clay both womb and shroud.

Fill your lungs
with the last burning air
with fetid terror.

Jettison your bones
leave them for diviners
or their clever dogs.

Learn to swim
with transparent limbs
a ghost through granite.

Go now, back
through earth's tight passage
to dark chaos, the spinning tomb.

Infirmary Visit

My always impeccably groomed mother
sits bare assed,
tied to a potty chair on wheels,
scant apron across her lap:
private parts
no longer private here.
Age has strip-mined her mind,
stretched the skin on her head skull-tight,
shriveled her body so thin the wedding ring
she wore for more than fifty years
slipped off her finger.

Front tooth chipped,
she gives me a hag's leer,
grabs my hand, begs
take me out of this place
anywhere

home. But home has suffered a diaspora:
the objects that defined her life
dispersed to nephew, niece, neighbour —
muffin tins, piano, embroidered
pillow cases —
a household hit by hurricane.

I spoon ice cream
between her gums;
she confides in me,
a stranger,   how hard
it is to mother a daughter
who expects too much,
demands that she
be perfect.

➤

Leaning in I whisper
but you were:

it was so easy
to leave in your hands the iron
you snatched from mine,
to leave to you the needles and pins,
scrub mop, the crack in the lid
of the flowered tea pot.

Jeff Seffinga

Starling Mind

They sit solid
battered by the storm

Rain beats at them
from all directions

They huddle
clinging to sturdy boughs
familiar and safe

Cold water
seeps with the wind
through their feathers

They shiver
tuck eyes and heads
tight under wings

Not one
decides

Now is the time
to fly away
against the wind

Chosen People

Only two years in this new land
I learned how we were chosen.
Skipping an afternoon of school, I hid
in a churchyard's cool shadow,
immigrant child among the gravestones
of Loyalist settlers so long dead,
and with wide eyes of innocence
watched my father at work.
In sun hot as an Egyptian desert,
under the dignified architect's direction
workmen built a wall.
The high line of red brick was urged
upward by hand and trowel,
levels and taut lines of twine.
Shouts of the bricklayers rang like bells
through my churchyard sanctuary.

My father shirtless with sweat running
like small streams in the dry dust
layered like desert sand on his back,
loaded bricks on a wooden frame.
When a builder called, he carried
the load aloft up a ladder:
a three-legged mule sent scrambling
on the cliff's steepest trail.
Or when one called for mortar
he filled a bucket, hung it from a pulley,
and with the practiced grace
of the bell-ringer at a cathedral carillon
he'd send the bucket skyward
and spill no drop.
He stood always tall, always alert
to every craftsman's call.

I knew then how the Hebrews built
those tombs at Pharaoh's will
and understood my father believed
for himself the promise God gave them:
This shall not last. The future belongs
to your children and their children's
children, for you are chosen.

And everywhere children's voices
ring among brick walls.

K.V. Skene

Tyneham

evacuated by the War Office in 1943
"for the duration of the Emergency"

Dead, even in the hearts of its few,
still-living exiles, these greystones
monument a lifetime alien and irrelevant
to armour-piercing, high explosive
and phosphorous tank shells fired
over Lulworth range — the war-world
now fills Tyneham valley. We are

pilgrims to a mock-up life — out of date
as if, in this ruin of a post office,
a care-wrapped parcel, long-promised letter
awaited a postman. We can tramp

Bronze Age barrows, find Celtic fields,
flint flakes, Samian ware, a coin of Commodus,
spot-check Saxon earthworks surrounded
by medieval lynchets. Ghosts walk here
and always have — but war

cut the tough thread tying life
to life, unfastened greystone homes
from snug slate roofs, snapped door-bolts,
broke windowpanes wide open
to strangers. Now-rained-upon hearths
have forgotten the slow burn of chilblains,
night-sweats, stillbirths, the too-familiar pain
of death — and the joy

of hay-filled barns, spring lambing time,
a Christmas Pantomime. St. Mary's church
purged of candle-wax, yellowed music
and not-so-fresh flowers. The school house
scoured of child-spilt ink, chalk dust,
and damp woolly jumpers. Rebuilt

to lay out leftovers of a village
sacrificed a wartime ago
that should be left to sink
like the small bones of rabbits
into the earth. Death

holds its own beauty — left alone
we all return home. Some kinds of love
take us places
we should not go.

St. Aldhelm's

A stone pilgrimage through fields
that grow green to gold to brown
season after season, into a low sun,
whitewashed cliffs — pale sails that splice
cold sea to sky. Ahead,
a greystone chapel collects
the devout, the curious, the totally
confused. A well-buttressed survivor
of damp, storm-shriven cattle
and twentieth-century war — resurrected
with a plough-found grave; a medieval
woman's bones. The open door
coaxes me in — I don't want
words, I speak to my god
with my life — yet here
in the almost dark, almost
alone, I whisper, "Come
closer. Help me
with love."

Deirdre Armes Smith

Meeting House at St. Helen's

Austere dissenters
breathed life into the walls
of this old place
now caught between the gas works
and a public house;
nor has it flickered out.
Faith that stood fast
three hundred years ago
against the gales of heresy
still haunts these stones.

Open the iron gate.
Walk down the row of flags.
Look upwards at the sundial,
Roman numerals glinting
in the uncertain light
and now and then observe
the shadow that the gnomon casts
whispering of times
far far removed from ours
when Quaker men and women
walked under it to pray
to their demanding god
who drove them without mercy
onto the rocks of silence.

Terraced House

Only a terraced house
at the row's end
with red and blue glass
in the front door,
like a thousand others.

But here inside
I am bewitched
by such a tender aura
that gives me back the birthright
fate had snatched away.

Low windows in the upstairs room
where once she sat
to see the lime tree bloom,
now brims with peace that fills
the black hole in my body.

And from the soft green
fireplace — tiles she chose
her unremembered voice
comes out to speak to me in tones
I always should have known.

Only a terraced house in a town street
from where she left to give me birth
and never more returned
until today, when her clear spirit
breathes comfort on my years of loss.

Prayer of an Islamic Woman

I only ask
to sit inside the doorway
with the sleeping child —
to see the future
through the veil
of his dark eyelashes.

I only ask
to wash his clothes
in the cool river
and hang them on the baking wall
where the green lizards
catch the sun's heat.

I only ask
to spoon the food
from the dark cooking pot
onto the man's plate
and see him fall on it
after a day in the fields,
like a starving dog.

I only ask
to lie down at night
between the child and the man —
to close my eyes
against the fierce moon,
without the noise of gunfire
or the dry fear of death.

John Souster

Farm Kitchen

In her farm kitchen with its rough, flagged floor
She salted pork, made bacon, brawn and lard;
On a scrubbed table, wrinkled as herself,
She kneaded dough, rolled pastry, mixed her cakes;
While through a door there stood a dairy slab,
A separator and a wooden churn
With bowls of buttermilk and cream and eggs.

So did she feed her household, so fed me
When nearly fifty years ago I came
In search of work, ill-nourished and alone.
All through a winter in the wind-swept fields
I lifted roots, hedged, ploughed and gathered strength,
But in the spring it was to this small church
Behind two horses that I followed her.

Somewhere beneath this grass, without a stone,
She lies at last; and I am moved to say,
Agnostic as I am, "God rest her soul."

Sandra Staas

Rusty Lines

We sit by the railway lines
stretching over to
Edinburgh City.
Words leap in the autumn afternoon
in heaps of orange
golden intrigue.
Warmed by the musty odour
we play hopscotch on
rusty sleepers.
Leap high over old stones,
become shooting stars
flying foolish.
Rebirth whisks its cycle,
a copper-hued track,
screeching battlefields.
We tumble as rockets
exploding on tracks,
ashes of gold,
spinning through dark
tunnels to arrive.

Jean Stanbury

Return to Culloden

I had not thought
to face again such shards of sleet
such thrashing rain — grim moorland ground
unchanged by time, dark peaty pools
rust-brown like blood.

to sense once more
the power of Butcher Cumberland's guns
black waves of rage, thick choking smoke
such hungering of steel for flesh
a dying cause.

to recognise
loyal courage of outnumbered clans
hot desperate thrust of clansmen's swords
their bitter charge through bayonets
to gutted death.

to realize
stark horror of uneven odds
the triumph of red-coated troops
in screaming charge — the aftermath
no mercy shown.

I had not thought
to pace again past Highland graves
no heather grows on those green mounds,
to face at last a cold grey stone
marked with my name,

tartan as shroud.

Andrew Stickland

At Peredelkino

The old train from Moscow leaves us
In the arms of a morning wind.
It is a spring full of cold sunshine
And the platform is quick to empty.

We have come to this place as pilgrims,
Following in the footsteps of pilgrims
Along the snow-lined road, up
To the cemetery at the turning of the road.

Boris Pasternak is buried here,
And we have come to pay our respects,
To seek our own inspirations
Among the stonework and the metalwork

And to remember his lonely words,
The words of a poem once banned, yet still
Recited from memory at his funeral
By those mourners, like us, gathered

In the late-spring snows, shuffling,
Stamping our feet against the cold,
Trying to be solemn while, unconcerned,
The villagers pass us by.

Thick-gloved fingers flick the pages
To find the same delicate words
And cast them forth into the frozen air,
To drift among the new green of the trees.

And when we are done with words
And silence, we retrace the steps
Of the mourners and the pilgrims, lost
in our own contemplations, to wait

In the dying sun of afternoon
For the old train back to Moscow.

Dorothy Stott

Inventions

1

Butterfly patterns poised on perfectly matched
paper wings
painted by the same hand
that created mountains.

2

Walking across sand I hear stones
calling my name
and the morning sunlight
melts their skins to glass.

3

These are the days of long shadows
and crimson skies
dripping bird songs
into late evening.

4

Summer rain drenches the passions
of thirsting lovers
their beloved faces
believe they can wash away stone.

George Swaney

Born Again Ex-Marine Reservist and a Big Woman in a Mu-Mu

have moved in next door. Now what do I do?

He "talks Bible" a lot. Nothing wrong with that
but I've heard it all before. God Bless America,
you know. But if that means the Federal Reserve Bank,
the Pentagon and Chrysler — well, doughnuts too.

I would rather hear about the Marines.
I've never *met* a Marine before, or
a Marine Reservist. Was he in Desert Storm, or
Sweep? Somehow we never get that far.

*

He helped me unpack groceries from my car
last week and preached about Ezekiel,
Jacob's Ladder, six-headed monsters.
I thought, "Great bloody yarblockos to you,
me bucko." But it's a free country.

*

Last Sunday I mowed the lawn and he
called me over to the fence. He was
shooting bow and arrows in his backyard.

I let the mower stall and walked to the fence.
He asked me about burning trash on Saturdays
then slid gracefully into Daniel's lion's den.
Then loaves and fishes, water into wine, devils
into swine, six-headed monsters. Spice Girls.

*

➤

It's summer so his wife sits on the porch.
She's a porch squatter. Pink plastic flyswatter.
Resemble? Brian Wilson c. 1976, but without
the beard. Do you know Brian Wilson?

Sitting in a car outside your house.
Remember when you spilled Coke all over your blouse?
T-shirt, cut-offs, and a pair of thongs.
We've been having fun all summer long.

*

I hate unpacking the car now or mowing
the lawn. But I always hated mowing the lawn.

Of course I want to say (but I can't, being me)
"I know all about Good Samaritans, 40 days
in the desert, plagues and locusts, Caesar Augustus,
fig leaves, fiery furnaces, Pharaohs.
But with the taxes I pay who gives a dirty doughnut?
I grew up on that stuff. You just heard it last year!"

*

Set the scene: archery set, camouflage hat,
200 lb. jellyroll on the porch, Bible talk.

Tell it to the Marines.

Lynn Tait

Hunting for Bear

It is hunting season.
My man worries.

He wishes I had broom-like bones,
feathered bristles
bending backwards
against cork and clapboard,
leaning into
clean, vacant corners,
clinging to
flour and flaxseed,
smelling of
cabbage and camphor.

He knows I wish to gaze upon the bear's head,
embrace its spirit.

He suspects this has already happened
and plies me with honey;
tries to make me dance,
hoping to
tame the bear.

Stephen Threlkeld

The Empire Builders of Broadbottom

I have seen
The white feathered goose
Seeking with outstretched beak
Over the barbed-wire fence,
With no thought
For the mill-race,
For the turn of the wheel,
Of a hundred years ago,
And the two thousand workers,
Driven by belts and pulleys,
Who built an empire.
Their grey houses in line
On the steep-sided street.
Where at Christmas
Sprigs of holly
From the hedges,
Were fastened to pictures
Of The Stag at Bay, or
The Lady of Shalott,
Hanging above the
Mahogany sideboard,
In the front room.
Now wild flowers grow
Where water once flowed,
And the ghosts of mill workers
Share the row houses
With managers, teachers and
Assorted Manchester intellectuals.
As dusk closes the day,
Soft yellow lights
Appear in four-paned windows.
And the dark-faced Swaledale sheep
Move to higher ground.

Hilary Tinsley

To My Son

Exhaustion hung on every limb.
I heard you scream
as snatched from your security
you shouted loud your loss.
Your cry released the spring of love.
Resentment gone,
devotion flooded through to wash
away my bitterness.
Too late to wish the act undone.
Extinguished flame rebuked my empty womb,
and pain derided my remorse.

The years, a wasteland of aborted life,
behind me now,
I welcome death's approach; and you,
who wait to meet with me,

will you forgive?

Lilka Trzcinska-Croydon

Schubert's Trio in B Flat

Enclosed in my red bedroom,
reading Robert Hass
who talks of small things near Big Sur,
I am inside a heart
where, vibrant as a Bonnard painting,
Schubert's *Trio in B Flat*
flows over me.

Tucked into the pine mirror frame
is Melanie's picture:
coral shirt, blond hair flowing.
Behind, Atlantic's white manes
tasting to her like Passover.
From the opposite side of the frame
gazes an angel from Niccolo di Buonaccorso's
"Coronation of the Virgin."

The violin swells,
piano notes scatter,
a merry dialogue.
The sonorous cello
tumbles both into night.

— Time for my morning swim?
But I have not mentioned my dream:
I was running along Piha beach
where my grandsons, Toby and Evan,
were building black sandcastles.
Amelia's tiny face
bright as Auckland harbour.

Notturno begins.
The violin sings love, love, love,
the piano runs along with kisses.
They embrace in a duet, notes scatter stars.
Through cello's passionate darkness,
like daisies unpetalled
my lost love and I
come together, triumphant,
a veil of sadness dissolving
in the final tones.

Minutes later I slide
into cool water.
Trio's notes tremble on the waves,
glisten in early morning sun.

Sandee Gertz Umbach

The Secret

They said you bled
right here
on the factory floor.
Wiped it up with stiff
restroom towels
that crinkled like construction paper
on the concrete.

Hunched over,
wiping in circles
while Carol and Ann came running;
asking what they could do
what it was
and you said "leave it alone,
I'll get it,"
in the same voice
you might have told your girls
to move away
from broken glass
on the kitchen floor.

And you stuffed
some more of the towels
and kleenex
from your purse
down your shirt
to the raw oozing spot
of your breast
and took your place in line.

Lifted, fastened, taped,
'til sweat beaded on your cheeks
and you didn't think
your arm would rise
and support the weight
of this tumor gone mad
and thought
            "this is money
for my children's future."

Bolted to the wall,
the time clock
punched out hours
you'd put in,
the dirty jokes
you'd take home
and never repeat.
Those last weeks,
you were still making lists;
a gift for that baby shower,
shop for a futon
for your daughter's dorm room.
So busy being silent,
you built a wall
around your body,
no one can look,
no one can touch.

➤

The first time
the doctor saw it
he cried.
And still, we don't know
what a woman of faith
thought staring back
at the sight of her fears
traveling down a stranger's face
and onto the bedsheets.

No one ever saw it again
except kindly hospice workers
who came to change dressings
and bandage
what they could.
It was a small comfort.
Something to look forward to.

Maureen Weldon

Make Up — And the Mirror

In the morning, I see myself
as the old woman — who
witched her life in wax.

As I stand bewildered — amongst
yesterday's waiting dishes,
and the morning news.

"Turn over the bands!" they say,
"music! music!"

Now my daughter fills the sink
with bubbles and long-locked hair.

Now my mother wants scrambled egg,
in bed, in bed . . .

And somewhere my lover
who sometimes calls for dinner

and eats me late at night.
In the moonlight, in the middle of the night.

No, I must not let the wax set:
or the perfume dry . . .

Joanna M. Weston

Cedar

the tide rises
clothing me green

I drink until cedar
flows my body

green lifting from
hands and eyes

cedar hangs lace
about my shoulders

I am tall, long-armed
and dark with rain

Andrena Zawinski

We Remember Skinning Chicken

We are skinning chicken in my mother's kitchen,
sticky wet in July. *We'll make soup from this,*
she says, wishing for rain. The blade flashes
along the pale slick of breast, rends
the first fat in a stream of blood down my arm.
That will be a scar, she says, *like mine, the one
I got from the kerosene lantern on the mining hat,
reading when candles were dear & electric was out.*

Skin slips through my fingers. I tell her
I remember things: a feather-ticked bed, her warmth
around me in winter under the tar paper roof
in the shingled shack. She says she can't remember
at 72, but then she remembers: her father, packing
his black bucket, water bottle on the bottom, fresh
slaughtered smoked sausage sandwiched
in warm baked bread at the top. She remembers
primping for a Jennerstown boy, rubbing
the smell of smoke & onion away with salt
when there wasn't enough milk for the babies. She says
Papa rode the buggy on the rail down the hole. He bit
the life out of land in Windber's #40, fed pig gristle
to rats who ran warnings when oxygen thinned
before sirens called a cave-in.

Skinny sinews slide through baubles of grease. I cut
my slippery hand again, ask her about the lantern light,
but she tells me about candles, taller than she was
at twelve, circling her young mother's coffin
and the Christmas tree planted in sawdust.
Rubbing her scar, *there was almost a fire,* she says,
when mama's first lover staggered in wailing.
Wincing back tears, she scoops the last glob
into a baggie. *When it cools off,* she says,
*during a nice rain, like my mother & I did,
we'll make soup from all this fat.*

Sleepless Night at Summer's End

Rockwood, Pennsylvania

The crickets can keep you awake
like an old rocking chair
loose on the rails.
The 10:45 CSX can slice the night,
scraping west from Altoona & howling
the bridge above Glade Run Creek
where Mohawk & Cree
once cut a path.

But what can a woman
do out in Rockwood?

She can put out salt lick & apples
for white-tailed deer,
pick a bouquet of goldenrod & sweet joe-pye
from uncut fields,
stake a roadside stand with odd bric-a-brac,
get her hair done at Bonnie's Salon
to have dinner down at McDivit's.
She can pull a daily wage
at Tinkey's lumber or the limestone works
in Milford or Somerset,
set up a satellite dish for city stars to come in;

but at night
alone in Rockwood,

she can't keep nosy moonlight
from creeping in the cracks
where she props a loaded shotgun
at the bedroom door, can't help thinking
a woman's scream
could be caught here
like a firefly in an airtight jar,
dulled by lightning at summer's end
storming the walls.

Afterword

Jim C. Wilson

By the time the entries to the Sandburg-Livesay Award had been narrowed down, my task was very difficult indeed. All the poems sent to me were readable and enjoyable, and every one contained evidence that a real poet was at work. James Deahl sent me John B. Lee's comments on People's Poetry: they include the statement, "The poem embraces the heart and mind and soul in one enfolding." In varying degrees, this was true of all the poems I considered.

But I couldn't split the prize among all of them! Careful reading and consideration managed to reduce my elite group to eighteen, and then to seven. Among the eighteen, there was much to admire. I wish I'd written, "all the buried hope / came crocusing up / like eggshells emptied by the birth of birds" ("Influenza Epidemic, 1918"). "Tyneham" was about a village evacuated in 1943, and finished brilliantly with: "Some kinds of love / take us places / we should not go."

Many of the poems were sad, but without being maudlin. A positive note was struck in "Afterlives," in which a carpet is lifted by a middle-aged couple to reveal a maple floor "as beautiful / as when we first moved in." As with their relationship, "only a little work / could make it glow." Good stuff!

I could go on and on, but read and enjoy the poems for yourself. My final seven included "Grace Notes," with its understanding of the richness and finiteness of love. "Lace" deals with loss of faith; the poem is clever but also true. "Tom's Will" is familiar territory for poets, but I like the references to the four elements, fire in particular. The phrase "black, ochre, cobalt, rust" almost seems to echo: earth, water, fire and air.

Honourable Mentions

"Kosovo" is sharp and concise; it is horrifying but there is no wanton wallowing in gore. It is admirably done, with a thought-provoking final stanza.

"Last Day" — every word resonates. Even Sam the dog is relevant to the drama. The emotions suggested by the final stanza are complex. When I read it I feel admiration — and panic.

Second Place

"I wear my mother's bones." What a title! Packed with music and whirling images. For a minute, I thought this poem might benefit from a soundtrack of marimbas, xylophones, wind chimes, etc. Then I realized the soundtrack is already there!

First Place

"Sentences." I liked and admired this poem from the start. At first it might seem simple, but with rereading, phrases develop layers of meaning. It is quiet and true, but with horror bubbling under.

My decision did, inevitably, involve my own tastes. Another judge might well have arrived at a different selection. To all the poets who didn't win, I have to say: I didn't reject you; it's just that, this time, I didn't select you.

The Poets

Becky D. Alexander lives in Cambridge (Ontario). Her work has won a first place and a second place in the Canadian Authors Association's literary contests for 1997 and 1998, respectively. She is the editor of *Paradise Poems*.

Winona Baker lives in Nanaimo (British Columbia). She was the International winner of the Basho Haiku Contest in 1989. Winona's books and chapbooks include: *Clouds Empty Themselves: Island Haiku, Not So Scarlet a Woman: Light and Humorous Poems, Moss-hung Trees: Haiku of the West Coast, Beyond the Lighthouse,* and *Wild Strawberries*. This is her third appearance in the annual Sandburg-Livesay anthology.

Jackie Bartley lives in Holland (Michigan), on the eastern shore of Lake Michigan. She is the author of two chapbooks: *When Prayer is Far From Our Lips* and *The Terrible Boundaries of the Body*, which won the White Eagle Coffee Store Press Chapbook Award for 1996. She was the runner-up in the 1998 Acorn-Rukeyser Chapbook Contest.

Theda Bassett lives in Murray (Utah).

Marion Beck, born and educated in Rossendale, England, now lives in Regina (Saskatchewan). She has twice been a winner in the People's Poetry Political Poem Contest, and was the winner of the Short Grain Prose Poem Contest in 1991. Her chapbooks are *Notebook of an Immigrant, Thin Grafts,* and *Poems for Amazons*.

Margaret Behr lives at Powell River (British Columbia). She is the author of a poetry chapbook, *Emma*, as well as the *Professional Manual for BC Massage Therapists*. She has also co-translated (with Robert Foster) Euripides' *Bacchae*.

Elinor Benedict, a native of Tennessee, splits her time between Rapid River (Michigan) and Naples (Florida). She was the co-winner of the Sandburg-Livesay Anthology Contest (1996) and has won several more awards for poetry, fiction, and journalism. She is the author of five poetry chapbooks: *Landfarer, A Bridge to China, The Green Heart, Chinavision,* and *The Tree Between Us* and the founding editor of *Passages North*, a literary magazine.

Ernest J. Berry lives in Picton (New Zealand). Born in Christchurch in 1929, he has been a cowboy/shepherd in the New Zealand high country, an importer-exporter of sewing machines, and a dune-buggying, frisbeeing poet on a remote Mexican beach. He is the author of an illustrated haiku book, *Raindrop*, and has had work in two of the Herb Barrett Award international haiku anthologies.

Karen Bodlak lives in New Westminster (British Columbia). In addition to having her poetry in literary journals, a number of her articles have appeared in *The Vancouver Sun*.

Laure-Anne Bosselaar lives in Cambridge (Massachusetts). Her poetry collection, *The Hour Between Dog and Wolf*, was published by BOA Editions. She edited *Outsiders: Poems about Rebels, Exiles, and Renegades* and co-edited (with her husband Kurt Brown), *Night Out: Poems about Hotels, Motels, Restaurants and Bars*. Her work has been nominated three times for the Pushcart Prize. She is currently translating Flemish poetry into English.

Brian Burke lives in Vancouver (British Columbia). His chapbook is *margaret atwood island* and his short fiction has appeared in *Stag Line: Stories by Men* (Coteau Books). This is Mr. Burke's third appearance in the annual Sandburg-Livesay Anthology.

Margo Button lives at Nanoose Bay (British Columbia). Her first poetry collection, *The Unhinging of Wings*, won The Dorothy Livesay Poetry Prize (1996). and was performed by Welcome Wood Productions, Kingston, Ontario. This is Ms. Button's second appearance in the annual Sandburg-Livesay anthology.

Terry Ann Carter was born in Cambridge (Massachusetts) and now lives in Nepean (Ontario), where she teaches high school. She has edited three collections of student poetry and art for General Store Publishing House. *Anapanasati,* her fifth chapbook, won second place in a contest sponsored by Cranberry Tree Press. *Waiting for Julia* has just been published, with royalties donated to the Canadian Relief Fund for Victims of Chernobyl in Belarus.

Marilyn Cay lives in Tisdale (Saskatchewan). She has received many awards, including the Saskatchewan Writers Guild Long Manuscript Award (1991), the Saskatchewan Writers Guild Short Fiction Award (1986), and the Saskatchewan Writers Guild Poetry Award three times (1987, 1990, 1994). Her work has appeared in half a dozen anthologies, most recently *What Is Already Known* and *In the Clear* (both Thistledown). She is the author of two titles: *Farm* and *Pure and Startled Seconds*.

Alison Chisholm was born in Liverpool and lives in Southport (Merseyside, England), where she serves as poetry and creative writing tutor at Southport College. She serves as poetry consultant to BBC Radio Merseyside. She has often won prizes in literary competitions, including overall winner of the American contests of the World Order of Narrative and Formalist Poets (1992). She is the editor of the Derbyshire volume in the *Poets' England* series. Her own verse has been published in seven collections, most recently *Daring the Slipstream*. This is Ms. Chisholm's second appearance in the annual Sandburg-Livesay anthology.

Denise Coney was born in Toronto in 1957 and now lives in a forest north of Toronto. She used to co-edit *Inkstone*. Her work has been anthologized, most recently in *Haiku Moment*.

Gloe Cormie lives in Winnipeg (Manitoba) and is a visual artist as well as a writer. She has won prizes in contests run by *Contemporary Verse 2* (for haiku) and *Prairie Fire* (for prose poetry), and her poems have been broadcast nationally on the CBC. Her work has appeared in the anthologies *The Six-Pack from Heaven* and *Potluck*.

Frank Correnti lives in Pittsburgh (Pennsylvania) where he edits *The Pittsburgh Quarterly* and is a long-time trade union activist. He served a judge of the Acorn-Rukeyser Chapbook Contest. Mr. Correnti contributed poetry to *Pittsburgh And Tri-State Area Poets*.

Terrance Cox was born in 1950 in northern Ontario. He has lived in Africa and at Bir Zeit in the West Bank, and currently resides in St. Catharines

(Ontario). As well as poetry, he writes journalism and plays. He has three collections to his credit: *In Local Orbit* (chapbook), *Backbeat* (audio cassette), and *Local Scores* (spoken word & music CD).

Barbara R. Crupi lives in Frating (Essex, England). She was born in 1943 in Suffolk. For over twenty years she was a partner with her husband on a family farm and she still maintains an extensive kitchen garden. Barbara's poetry has been broadcast on BBC and widely anthologized. Her collections are *Shadow Chasing, The Well Pool,* and *Before the Winter Comes.* This is her third appearance in the annual Sandburg-Livesay anthology.

Sandra Dempsey lives in Calgary (Alberta). She is the youngest of twelve, having been born into a solid Irish Celtic family. In addition to being a poet, she is an award-winning playwright, her drama being widely anthologized. Most recently, *Armagideon,* which had earlier won the Alberta Playwriting Competition, won the grand prize in Firefly Productions' International New Play Search, 1999.

Ernest Dewhurst lives in Lathom, near Skelmersdale (Lancashire, England). He had a farm childhood in the Pennines and was subsequently a journalist with the *Northern Daily Telegraph* and the *Guardian* (Manchester). He is the author of one poetry collection.

Shaheen F. Dil lives in Pittsburgh (Pennsylvania) where she is Senior Vice President, Portfolio Development, at PNC Bank, having previously served as a Vice President in Mellon Bank's Global Corporate Banking Dept. She holds a Ph.D. in International Relations from Princeton University, and publishes and lectures widely in the fields of political science and international relations, as well as giving poetry readings in the U.S. and in Germany.

Gerald England lives in Gee Cross, at the edge of the Pennines (England). with his lace-making wife, a son, and a Manchester terrier. He has been active in the small press scene for almost 30 years and edits the magazine *Aabye.* Eleven collections of his poems have been published: *Poetic Sequence for five voices; Mousings; The Wine the Women and the Song; For Her Volume One; Meetings; At the Moor's Edge; The Rainbow and Other Poems; Daddycation; Futures* (with Christine England); *Stealing Kisses; Four Square Replay,* and *Limbo Time.* He is a member of Cyberscribers, a international Internet writers' group (newhope@iname.com   www.nhi.clara.net/gehome.htm) This is Mr. England's second appearance in the annual Sandburg-Livesay anthology.

Janice Faria lives in Pittsburgh (Pennsylvania) and works at the Women's Center and Shelter of Greater Pittsburgh. Her work has appeared in *Pittsburgh And Tri-State Area Poets.*

Penny L. Ferguson lives in Truro (Nova Scotia) where she edits *The Amethyst Review.* In addition to poetry, she writes short stories and draws in ink. She is a member of the Writer's Council of the Writers' Federation of Nova Scotia and was writer-in-residence at Nova Scotia Teachers' College for three years. She is a contributor to *SEEDS: 12 Canadian Poets* and her own poetry collection is *Runaway Suite: Two Voices.* This is Ms. Ferguson's second appearance in the annual Sandburg-Livesay anthology.

Rina Ferrarelli lives in Pittsburgh (Pennsylvania) where she writes and translates (from the Italian) full time. Her two volumes of translations are: *I Saw the Muses* by Giorgio Chesura and *Light Without Motion* by Leonardo Sinisgalli. Her own poetry collections are *Home is a Foreign Country* and *Dreamsearch*. She has been awarded the Italo Calvino Prize. Ms. Ferrarelli has contributed poetry to *Pittsburgh And Tri-State Area Poets* and several textbook anthologies.

Lori C. Fraind lives in Reston (Virginia), where she writes poetry, stories, and creates illustrations, as well as working as a multimedia designer. A winner of many awards and prizes, she has received a PEN Women Award for versatility in writing.

Janet Fraser grew up in Halifax, lived in Toronto for many years, and now resides in St. John's (Newfoundland). A professional librarian, she writes book reviews and essays for newspapers and for CBC Radio.

Michael Fraser was born in Grenada, and has lived in Canada since the age of five. A graduate of York University, he lives in Toronto and edits *Sapodilla*. His work has appeared in the anthology *Seed*. This is his second appearance in the annual Sandburg-Livesay anthology.

Elizabeth Gourlay was born in Toronto, spent her childhood in New Brunswick, and lives in Vancouver (British Columbia). She has four books of poetry to her credit: *Motions, Dreams and Aberrations; Songs & Dances; M Poems; and Colours for Scriabin: New and Selected Poems*. She has also published a volume of short stories, *Celluloid Barrette*. She also writes plays — *The Glass Bottle, Isabel, The Cut Off, No Recourse, The Hair of the Dog* — and has seen them produced in Canada and the U.S. Her poems have appeared in many Canadian anthologies, including *Poetry by Canadian Women* (Oxford).

Mary Elizabeth Grace was born at Burke's Falls by the waters of Doe Lake, Ontario. She currently lives in Montreal. Nature, music, and her Irish-Hungarian heritage are inspirations. She is a co-founder of a four-author multicultural collective, which has recently published *Crossroads Cant*. Her book is *Bootlegging Apples on the Road to Redemption*. This is Ms. Grace's second appearance in the annual Sandburg-Livesay anthology.

Archie Greene lives and writes in Iowa City (Iowa). Although her name belies it, Archie is a female African-American. She suffers from spinal-cerebellar degeneration, a kind of ataxia.

Jay Harding is originally from Texas, but now lives in Pleasant Hill (California). His *Teardrops On The Counter* took first place in the Poetry Society of Texas and Lucidity Poetry Journal contest (1997). In 1993 he was named Poet of the Year by the Austin Poetry Society. His other poetry collections are *Waking Up In Ireland, Gypsy Spirit*, and, for children, *Tickle My Heart*. He is also a chemist and contributes to scientific and technical journals.

Gillian Harding-Russell — see page 149.

Irene Blair Honeycutt lives in Charlotte (North Carolina) where she teaches creative writing at Central Piedmont Community College. Her poetry book *It Comes As a Dark Surprise* won Sandstone Publishing's New South Poetry Series Contest (1992).

Susan Ioannou lives in Toronto (Ontario) where she is Director of Wordwrights Canada. She runs The Poetry Tutorial correspondence course and has produced *The Crafted Poem: A Step by Step Guide to Writing and Appreciation, Polly's Punctuation Primer, Ten Ways to Tighten Your Prose,* and *Writing Reader-friendly Poems: Over 50 Rules of Thumb for Cleaner Communication.* She was the founding editor of the annual *Canadian Writers' Contest Calendar* (now published by Mekler & Deahl). She is the author of a children's novel, *A Real Farm Girl,* and six poetry collections: *Motherpoems, Familiar Faces/Private Griefs, Spare Words, Clarity Between Clouds: Poems of Midlife,* and *Where the Light Waits.*

Kasara lives in Laconia (New Hampshire). Born after the A-bomb, she looks forward to the poetry of the third millennium. Performance poetry has taken her across North America and Europe. Her publications include *Water Rhythms* and *Synapse Shots* This is Kasara's second appearance in the annual Sandburg-Livesay anthology.

Earl Keener lives in Bethany (West Virginia) and works on the track gang at Weirton Steel.

Larry Kimmel was born in 1940 in Johnstown (Pennsylvania) and lives in Colrain (Massachusetts). He holds degrees from Oberlin Conservatory and the University of Pittsburgh and has worked at everything from steel mills to libraries. He has two poetry collections, *Lights Across The River* and *alone tonight,* as well as a novel, *A Small Silent Ordeal.*

Philomene Kocher lives in Kingston (Ontario). Her interests include writing haiku and exploring voice. This is Ms. Kocher's second appearance in the annual Sandburg-Livesay anthology.

Ken Kowal lives in Winnipeg (Manitoba). His first poetry chapbook, *i dream my father's hands,* was short-listed for the Heaven Chapbook Prize in 1997. A poet, singer, and song writer, he is a member of a poets' group that has produced two chapbooks, *The Six-Pack from Heaven,* and *Potluck.*

Joan Latchford was born in 1926 but did not begin writing until 1993. She lives in Toronto (Ontario) where she edits *Poemata* and publishes chapbooks under her Micro Prose imprint. She is a noted photographer. Her poetry chapbook is *Pearly Gates and other separations.* A second collection, *The Streets Where I Live,* is due out later this year. This is Ms. Latchford's second appearance in the annual Sandburg-Livesay anthology.

John B. Lee lives in Brantford (Ontario). He was born in 1951 and was raised on a farm. He is the only poet to win the Milton Acorn Memorial People's Poetry Award twice (1993 & 1995). He also is a winner of the Tilden Canadian Literary Award for Poetry (CBC Radio/*Saturday Night*) and several other prizes. He is the editor of *That Sign of Perfection,* a collection of hockey poems and stories. His 26 books and chapbooks (mostly poetry) are: *Poems Only a Dog Could Love, Love Among the Tombstones, To Kill a White Dog, Fossils of the Twentieth Century, Broken Glass, Hired Hands, Small Worlds, The Day Jane Fonda Came to Guelph, Rediscovered Sheep, The Bad Philosophy of Good Cows, The Pig Dance Dreams, The Hockey Player Sonnets, When Shaving Seems Like Suicide, Variations on Herb, The Art of Walking Backwards, All The Cats Are Gone, What's in a name?,*

These Are the Days of Dogs and Horses, Head Heart Hands Health: A History of 4-H in Ontario, The Beatles Landed Laughing in New York, Tongues of the Children, In a Language with no Word for Horses, Never Hand Me Anything if I'm Walking or Standing, Soldier's Heart, The Echo of Your Works Has Reached Me, and *Stella's Journey.* This is his third appearance in the annual Sandburg-Livesay anthology.

Norma West Linder was born in Toronto but spent her formative years on Manitoulin Island. She lives in Sarnia (Ontario). She is the author of five novels. Her eight volumes of poetry are *On the Side of the Angels, Pyramid, Ring Around the Sun, The Rooming House, This Age of Reason, Matter of Life and Death, Morning Child,* and *Jazz in the Old Orange Hall.* Ms. Linder has also written a memoir of Manitoulin Island, a children's book, and a biography of Pauline McGibbon. She was on the faculty of Lambton College, teaching English and creative writing, for twenty-four years.

Tanis MacDonald lives in Winnipeg (Manitoba) with too many books and not enough . . . She won the Acorn-Rukeyser Chapbook Contest with her first poetry collection, *This Speaking Plant.* (She lived for several years in Toronto where her poetry readings are legendary.) This is Ms. MacDonald's second appearance in the annual Sandburg-Livesay anthology.

Carol L. MacKay was born in 1964 in Tofield, grew up in Ryley, and currently lives in Bawlf (all in Alberta). After graduating from the University of Alberta she worked for twelve years in academic libraries. She has published both poetry and short stories in North American journals.

Joy Hewitt Mann lives in Spencerville (Ontario) where she runs a junkstore. She won the LaPointe Prize last year with her poem "My Father's Apple Orchard" and she also received the Leacock Award for Poetry the year before. A founding member of Ottawa's Valley Writers' Guild, her chapbook is *Voices From The Other Side of The Moon.*

Susan McCaslin lives in Port Moody (British Columbia). She teaches English and creative writing at Douglas College. Her poetry collections are *Locutions, Light Housekeeping, Veil/Unveil,* and *Letters to William Blake.* She edited *A Matter of Spirit: Recovery of the Sacred in Contemporary Canadian Poetry.*

Bruce Meyer was born in Toronto (Ontario) and teaches at the University of Toronto, where he runs the creative writing program. He is the author of five poetry collections — *The Tongues Between Us, The Aging of America, The Open Room, Radio Silence,* and *The Presence* — as well as various studies and profiles of Canadian writers. He edited *Arrivals: Canadian Poetry in the Eighties, Selected Poems of Frank Prewett,* and *Other Names for the Heart: Selected Poems of David Wevill.* Dr. Meyer, who often lectures on CBC Radio on The Great Books, will deliver the annual Milton Acorn Lecture at McMaster University later this year.

Renee Norman lives in Coquitlam (British Columbia) where she is a writer and part-time teacher, currently completing her doctorate. She won the *Whetstone* poetry contest in 1997. Her work has appeared in the anthologies: *Teaching to Wonder* and *Twenty-Five Years of Peace.*

H.F. Noyes lives in Attikis (Greece) and is the author of seven books of poetry and haiku.

R.U. Outavit loves to attend poetry readings and believes that to hear the voice of the poet can be a life-sustaining experience. He is a founding member of Fire of Prometheus, the legendary poetry performance troupe that originated the poetry slam style of reading. R.U.'s third volume of poetry, *Harmony Blossoms,* was nominated for the Pulitzer Prize in 1989. His long poem, *No Kids — Politically Incorrect/Borderline Gross,* to be released in 1999, promises to give the critics something to squawk about. Celebrated every year on July 14 since 1982, R.U. Outavit Day honours poetry's contributions to World Peace; the 1999 celebration took place in Dayton, Ohio. http://www.walnuthills.com/ This is R.U.'s second appearance in the annual Sandburg-Livesay anthology.

William Oxley was born in Manchester in 1939 and lives in Brixham (Devon, England). A poet and philosopher, he has also worked as a part-time gardener an accountant, and an actor. His many collections of verse include *The Dark Structures, New Workings, Passages from Time, The Icon Poems, Opera Vetera, Mirrors of the Sea, Fightings, Eve Free, The Mundane Shell, Superficies, Wind, The Exile, The Notebook of Hephaestus, A Map of Time, The Triviad, The Mansands Trilogy, Mad Tom on Tower Hill, The Hallsands' Tragedy, Forest Sequence, The Patient Reconstruction of Paradise, The Play Boy, In The Drift Of Words, Cardboard Troy, Collected Longer Poems,* and *The Green Crayon Man.* He has edited or co-edited nine British literary reviews, most recently *Acumen.* His translation of the poetry of L.S. Senghor, *Poems of a Black Orpheus,* appeared in 1996. He is a former member of the General Council of the Poetry Society and founder of the Long Poem Group.

Margaret Pain lives in Woking (Surrey, England) where she was born. She spent most of her working life in business, "finding" modern poetry in her forties. Since 1978 she has been a co-editor of *Weyfarers* and for many years served as assistant editor of *Envoi.* She was Deputy Chairman or Chairman of the Surrey Poetry Centre and Wey Poets for many years. Her poetry has won several prizes, including the New Poetry Competition and the Surrey Poetry Centre Open Competition. She has written four chapbook collections: *Walking to Eleusis, No Dark Legend, A Fox in the Garden,* and *Shadow Swordsman.* This is her third appearance in the annual Sandburg-Livesay Anthology.

Kathy Pearce-Lewis was born in New York, raised in Colorado, and lives in Bethesda (Maryland), where she is a long-time members of The Writer's Center. Her poetry has appeared in several anthologies: *Rye Bread, Second Rising, Free State, The Cooke Book,* and *Poetry at the Angel.* She is a linguist and an enthusiastic birder.

Ruth Roach Pierson lives in Toronto (Ontario) where she teaches women's history and feminist studies at the Ontario Institute for Studies in Education, University of Toronto. She hopes to retire soon and devote herself full time to poetry and her cat Haiku.

Peggy Poole — see page 148.

Joan Poulson lives in Sale, near Manchester (England), where she writes poetry and prose for both adults and children. She is the author of 16 titles treating traditional and regional English food, traditional festivals, and local customs and has been writer-in-residence with a modern dance company, an art gallery, a museum, and a psychiatric hospital. Her children's verse has been collected into almost a hundred anthologies on four continents. Her publications are *earthbeing*, *Girls Are like Diamonds*, *Celebrations*, and *Pictures in my Mind*.

Jeff Seffinga, a poet from Hamilton (Ontario), has tried all his life to escape his peasant roots. Although he aims for a life of leisure and nobility, he has only managed to join the working class. He edited two anthologies published by Mekler & Deahl, *Ingots* and *A Cliff Runs Through It*. His own poetry collections are *Three Crows Flying*, *Lunatic Hands*, *Tight Shorts*, and *Bailey's Mill*.

K.V. Skene is a long-term expat Canadian living in Swanage (England), a small seaside town in Dorset. Her books/chapbooks are *Pack Rat, fire water*, and *The Uncertainty Factor/As A Rock*. This is Ms. Skene's third appearance in the annual Sandburg-Livesay anthology.

Deirdre Armes Smith has lived in Worsley (Manchester, England) all her life. She is the author of seven books: *Cycles of the Moon*, *Church Bells on a Wet Sunday*, *Winter Tennis Courts*, *The Real Thing*, *With Untold Care*, *Mother of Wales*, *Drawn by the Moon*, and *Invisible Lady*. Her work has appeared in several anthologies, including *Marigolds Grow Wild on Platforms* (edited by Peggy Poole) and *The Poet's England*. She has won prizes in the Julia Cairns Competition and the Southport Writers Open Competition. This is her third appearance in the annual Sandburg-Livesay anthology.

John Souster lives in Wallingford (Oxon, England). He was born in Northampton in 1912 but grew up in New Zealand. He is a retired horticulturist and a World War II vet. Mr. Souster's poetry collection is *Looking Before and After*. This is his third appearance in the annual Sandburg-Livesay anthology (he received an Honourable Mention in 1996 for his poem "To John Clare").

Sandra Staas grew up in Scotland and lived in Spain for many years before settling in Coraopolis (Pennsylvania). Her poetry has appeared in *The Pittsburgh Quarterly* and other reviews.

Jean Stanbury lives in West Kirby (Wirral, England). Of Scottish descent, her love of Scotland is reflected in much of her poetry. Her poems have been broadcast on BBC Northwest, have appeared in a number of anthologies, and have won her several prizes. Her poetry collection is *Winged Seeds*.

Andrew Stickland lives in London (England) where he works at the National Theatre. He was born in Forres (Scotland) in 1966, but spent much of his life in Lincolnshire. Andrew studied law at University College, London. He has three collections: *Broken Bottles*, *The Opposite Page,* and *Mathematical Love*. This is his third appearance in the annual Sandburg-Livesay anthology.

Dorothy Stott was born in England and came to Canada in 1966. She now lives in Gibson (British Columbia). She has won the Alberta Scouten Memorial Award, first prize in the Suncoast Forge Literary Competition, and second prize in the Hope Writers' Poetry Competition and the Alberta Poetry Competition. This is her second appearance in the annual Sandburg-Livesay anthology.

George Swaney lives in Uniontown (Pennsylvania) but is imoving to New Mexico. He has published work in *The Pittsburgh Quarterly* and other reviews.

Lynn Tait was born in Toronto in 1956. She resides in Sarnia (Ontario). Her poetry has appeared in *People's Poetry Letter* and other journals.

Stephen Threlkeld, a retired professor of biology, lives in Hamilton (Ontario). He grew up on the Atlantic coast of Cornwall (U.K.) and came to North America in 1951 to farm. Later he attended the University of Alberta (agriculture) and then returned to England to continue his studies at Cambridge University, where he obtained his doctorate in plant genetics. He enjoys camping, T'ai Chi, and kayaking. His poems appeared in *A Cliff Runs Through It* (Mekler & Deahl).

Hilary Tinsley lives in Southport (Merseyside, England) with her husband and three sons. She teaches children with learning difficulties. Her poems have appeared in a number of anthologies in the U.K. and have been broadcast on BBC Northwest.

Lilka Trzcinska-Croydon was born in Poland in 1925. She and her family were arrested by the Gestapo in 1943 for involvement in the Resistance. Her mother died in Auschwitz, but her father, brother, and two sisters survived. After her liberation in 1945 from Bergen-Belsen, where she had been transferred, she went to Italy, and the next year to England. In 1948 she moved to Toronto (Ontario), where she now lives. Lilka is a psychoanalytic child therapist in private practice. She writes in both Polish and English; other interests include painting, travel, cinema, Greek drama, and mythology. This is her second appearance in the annual Sandburg-Livesay anthology.

Sandee Gertz Umbach lives in McMurray (Pennsylvania). She is the mother of two young sons. She writes a weekly column for the *Washington Observer-Reporter* and her poems and essays have appeared in *The Pittsburgh Quarterly*. In 1998 she was nominated for a Pushcart Prize for her work in poetry.

Maureen Weldon lives in Saltney (Chester, England). An Irishwoman and a former dancer with the Irish Theatre Ballet Company, her poetry is heard on Radio Merseyside. She is the author of several poetry titles: *Leap, No Pawns In This Play, Of Crossed Wires*, and, most recently, *Divided*. She and her daughter, Karina, are great friends. This is Ms. Weldon's second appearance in the annual Sandburg-Livesay anthology.

Joanna M. Weston was born in England and lives in Prince Albert (Saskatchewan). She and her accountant husband have three sons and one cat, and are currently renovating a house and a garden. Her four chapbooks are *One of These Little Ones, Cuernavaca Diary, Seasons,* and *All Seasons*.

Andrena Zawinski teaches and writes in Pittsburgh (Pennsylvania). Her poetry collection, *Traveling in Reflected Light,* won the Kenneth Patchen Book Competition in 1996. Ms. Zawinski has twice been nominated for a Pushcart Prize, and she was named the One-to-Watch in Literature by *Pittsburgh Magazine* in its inaugural Excellence in the Arts Awards. Her work has appeared in *Pittsburgh And Tri-State Area Poets*.

Peggy Poole

My own definition of poetry — a pattern of words compressing emotion, experience, or thought into its own energy — fails to convey how a poem can change lives. Dannie Abse tells of an Irish poet who said, we "should come to a poem sober and leave it drunk." In the language of the Haida tribe, I'm told, the verb for making poetry is the same as the verb to breathe. I find that wonderful.

For me, poetry is a consuming passion, a ruling factor. I've been fortunate through my work with the BBC to be able to offer many poets air time. A great privilege. I write from anger, hurt, love, curiosity, bewilderment — whatever. If a subject is personal I try to craft it so that it embraces a wide range; conversely, if I'm writing about a character from history or literature, I need to find some element that resonates with my own being. Once a poem grabs me it won't let go until it's done, no matter how long that may take. Later comes the tightening with my three S's as guidelines: specify, scissors, and sing. But I know no magic formula for immortality.

Born on a farm in Kent, Peggy Poole has spent most of her life living on the shores of the Dee looking out to the Welsh mountains. She now lives in West Kirby, Merseyside. An author, journalist, and broadcaster, she recently retired as poetry consultant to BBC North's *Write Now*. Much published in poetry magazines, Peggy, a frequent adjudicator, is currently a regular columnist for *Writing* and *Writers News*, and tutor for their correspondence poetry course. She has edited several anthologies, including *Windfalls, Poet's England: Cumbria,* and *Marigolds Grow Wild on Platforms*. She has written several children's books and an adult novella. Her poetry publications are *Never a Put-up Job, Cherry Stones and other poems, No Wilderness in Them, Midnight Walk, Hesitations, Trusting the Rainbow, Bruised, Rich Pickings,* and, most recently, *From the Tide's Edge*.

Gillian Harding-Russell

A poem creates its own form. It finds its own rules, whether choosing to meet the requirements of traditional verse, inventing its own rules, or a combination. Rather than following linear logic or narrative, a poem radiates meaning on various levels. Often, a poem starts as a snippet of ordinary language, but magically goes beyond to imply a larger framework or an alternate ironic reference. Words, combined in unusual ways and wrenched beyond the uses of common speech, transcend everyday contexts.

Since a poem concentrates meaning, is a long poem a contradiction in terms? No, I think not. Maps and poems necessarily come with their own scales and code, which the sympathetic reader must decipher. In a poem's centrifugal shape, it has the intricacy of a flower or even of a cancerous cell. And a longer poem might be said to have the power and range of a supernova or of a larger area of cancerous metastasis. Poems may be celebratory but not always. A poem often entertains negative feelings but, in so doing, one hopes, exorcises them. The act of expression in itself remains an affirmation.

Every poem's genesis is, of course, slightly different. I began "I wear my mother's bones" as that phrase stuck in my head and gathered a life of its own. Typically such lines come to me when I'm bothered and can't sleep or I wake up disturbed or I'm just crashingly bored and looking for an imaginative diversion. Or I may start with some image that somehow encapsulates a feeling or fear, ephemeral and un-pin-down-able, that has been getting under my skin. When I write that phrase or image down, related words and images spring to mind, and the poem evolves its own peculiar language and structures for meaning. But I don't often know what I mean, at least not very clearly, until I write it out.

Equinox (March, 1999) reports the discovery by Rachel Mayberry at McGill that stutterers typically stop using their hands when their speech fails, suggesting a physiological relation between language and the hands that may partly explain why people often benefit from writing it out. I always write a poem longhand first, to get over the initial "stuttering," only later resorting to a word processor to work out the details.

Gillian Harding-Russell lives in Regina, Saskatchewan. She has had poetry published in magazines across Canada. Her chapbook is *At the End of the Garden* (Green, 1990). She has been poetry editor for *Event* since 1989.

Contest judge

Jim C. Wilson

Jim C. Wilson is a Scottish poet, short-story writer, and creative-writing tutor. He did not begin writing seriously until he was in his thirties.

Jim was born in Edinburgh in 1948. He was largely unaffected by poetry at school, which he left in 1966 to begin a career in insurance. A fascination with words developed through his love of music, and he took an increasing interest in the lyrics of such artists as Tim Hardin, Phil Ochs, Leonard Cohen, and Scotland's own Incredible String Band.

Uninspired by updated pension schemes, he studied English Language and Literature at Edinburgh University (graduating with an MA (Hons) in 1971), where he found himself enjoying Wordsworth, Tennyson, Hardy, and Yeats. He taught English and Communication at Edinburgh's Telford College for nine years. It was only when tiredness and disillusionment set in that he decided to make a go of becoming a full-time writer. With the support of his wife Mik, whom he'd married in 1971, he left Telford College (and security) in September 1981.

Publication and recognition were not immediate. Jim knew about English but he still had to learn to be a writer. He persevered and eventually was awarded two Scottish Arts Council bursaries, and became Writing Fellow for Stirling District.

Although he has had a number of stories published and broadcast, and has co-written a biography (which became a radio series) of the eccentric Scottish entrepreneur, Howard Denton. Jim's main work has become his poetry. Over fifteen years, his poems have been featured extensively in magazines, journals, newspapers, and anthologies.

He has done well in U.K. competitions. He won the Swanage Arts Festival Literature Competition three times, and in 1997 was awarded the Hugh MacDiarmid Trophy. His sonnet "At Edlingham Church" received an honourable mention in the 1996 Sandburg-Livesay Anthology Contest.

His two published collections are *The Loutra Hotel* (Making Waves Press) and *Cellos in Hell* (Chapman). His poems have been described as "subtle yet unpretentious, humorous yet realistic" (Tessa Ransford) and as "technically accomplished and highly readable ... unflinching ... grittily contemporary" (Mario Relich, *Lines Review*).

Since 1994 he has been running Poetry in Practice sessions at Edinburgh University.

In 1998, at the age of 50, Jim, with Mik, left Edinburgh to go and live in the peaceful East Lothian village of Gullane, near an unspoiled seacoast of huge dunes and golden beaches. However, he enjoys travel, and has been frequently to Greece; he also loves France, Spain, and Amsterdam.

He has a passion for the music of Elvis Presley, and once drank malt whiskey with James Deahl in Edinburgh, at midnight, in the middle of a river.

Acknowledgements

Theda Bassett's "Saw Mill in Dry Creek Canyon" was first published in *Byline*.

Elinor Benedict's "Chinese Puzzle" was collected in her chapbook *Chinavision*. Her "In a Far City" was first published in *Helicon Nine*.

Laure-Anne Bosselaar's four poems "A Paris Blackbird", "English Flavors", "August", and "The Feather at Breendonck" are reprinted from her book *The Hour Between Dog and Wolf* (BOA Editions).

Brian Burke's "pocket knife" was first published in *Carousel*. His "the train through the far northwest" first appeared in *Northward Journal*.

Terry Ann Carter's "Calling Out the Beautiful Names" and "Belarus" have been collected in her book *Waiting for Julia* (Third Eye).

Marilyn Cay's "heavy old red Buick and K.T. Oslin and I" was first published in *Grain*.

Ernest Dewhurst's "Storm Lamp" have been accepted for a collection of his work due later this year from The National Poetry Foundation.

Penny L. Ferguson's "Legacy Of Shadows" was first published in *Canadian Author*. It was later collected in her book *Runaway Suite: Two Voices* (Hidden Brook Press).

Rina Ferrarelli's "The Streetcar" was first published in *Ball State University Forum*. Her "The Bricklayers" appeared in *VIA — Voices in Italian Americana* as well as in the *Pittsburgh Post-Gazette*. And the poem "Afterlives" was first published in *College English*.

Earl Keener's "Right Field Lines" and "Wallflower" were first published in *West Branch*.

Ken Kowal's "song of the butcher" and "i dream my father's hands" were published in his chapbook collection *i dream my father's hands*.

John B. Lee's "The Woman with the Hem of Her Coat Hanging" and "Influenza Epidemic, 1918" will be included in his forthcoming poetry collection, *Stella's Journey* (Black Moss Press).

Renee Norman's "In Benign Remembrance" was first published in *Whetstone*.

William Oxley's "Omaha Beach, 6th June 1944" was first published in *The Swansea Review*. His "The White Table, 4 a.m." first appeared in *Acumen*.

Margaret Pain's "Millerground, Windermere" was first published in *Country Life*. The poem was later collected in her book *Shadow Swordsman* (Envoi Poets Publications)

Kathy Pearce-Lewis' "For a Lost Miner" was first published in *Dog River Review*.

K.V. Skene's "Tyneham" was first published in the anthology *Dorset Contours* and later in *Deus Loci: The Lawrence Durrell Journal*. Her "St. Aldhelm's" first appeared in *AABYE (New Hope International)*.

Andrena Zawinski's "We Remember Skinning Chicken" was first published in *The Pittsburgh Quarterly*. Her "Sleepless Night at Summer's End" first appeared in the *Pittsburgh Post-Gazette*.

About Carl Sandburg

Carl Sandburg (1878–1967) worked at many jobs — day laborer, hobo, dishwasher, soldier, farm hand, and newspaper reporter — before publishing his first volume of poetry at the age of almost forty years. His poetry titles include *Chicago Poems; Cornhuskers; Smoke and Steel; Slabs of the Sunburnt West; Good Morning, America; The People, Yes; Honey and Salt; Breathing Tokens; Billy Sunday and Other Poems;* and *Poems for the People.* Sandburg twice won the Pulitzer Prize for poetry. He won a third Pulitzer for his history of Abraham Lincoln's Civil War years. All told, over thirty books of poetry, fiction, non-fiction, and children's literature bear his name.

In addition to his work for daily newspapers in Chicago, Sandburg also wrote for the *International Socialist Review* and *The Masses.* He founded what Selden Rodman called Proletarian Poetry (now better known as Populist Poetry) and inspired many of the poets who came onto the American scene during the 1930s, such as Muriel Rukeyser, Kenneth Fearing, and the Benét brothers.

A realist who always had a broad romantic streak, Sandburg never surrendered his faith in the basic goodness of the People. His poetry was therefore noted for its rock-hard strength as well as its drifting-fog tenderness. At the time of his death he was America's favorite poet.

About Dorothy Livesay

Dorothy Livesay (1909–1996) had a remarkable seventy-year literary career. Livesay was a leading People's Poet, literary editor, magazine publisher, mentor, feminist, and social justice activist. She was one of the first poets in Canada to write about Marxism, the lives of working people, and women's sexuality. She also took on the taboo subject of aging as she herself grew older. In fact, there was no subject Livesay was afraid to tackle. While she was still an undergraduate at the University of Toronto, Livesay took on campus sexism and the academic establishment. And while active in the League of Canadian Poets she took on professional and academic elitism. She was a supporter of gay and lesbian rights when almost no one else was.

With her third and fourth books — *Day and Night* (1944) and *Poems for People* (1947), both Governor General's Award winners — she set the tone for People's Poetry in Canada. Indeed, much of the poetry written during the 1950s, '60s, and '70s was inspired by her example. Livesay's influence can be seen in the work of such poets as Margaret Atwood, Milton Acorn, and Rhea Tregebov. Her selected poems, *The Self-Completing Tree,* is a definitive work. An overview of her life work is presented in the posthumous *Archive for Our Times.* Her strong words and stronger deeds are missed by all who love Canadian poetry.

Other Books by Unfinished Monument Press/ hamilton haiku press / Mekler & Deahl, Publishers

Poetry

Milton Acorn, *To Hear the Faint Bells:*
　haiku, senryu and short poems from Canada's national poet
Milton Acorn & Cedric Smith, *The Road to Charlottetown*
Becky D. Alexander (editor), *Paradise Poems:*
　haiku from Cootes Paradise
Herb Barrett, *The Light Between*
Fred Cogswell (editor), *Doors of the Morning*
　The 1996 Sandburg-Livesay Award
James Deahl, *Blackbirds*
James Deahl (editor), *Mix Six*
James Deahl (editor), *The Northern Red Oak:*
　poems for and about Milton Acorn
Simon Frank, *Imaginary Poems*
LeRoy Gorman (editor), *Gathering Light*
　The 1996 Herb Barrett Award
Albert W.J. Harper, *Poems of Reflection*
John B. Lee, *The Echo of Your Words Has Reached Me*
Tanis MacDonald, *This Speaking Plant*
　The 1996 Acorn-Rukeyser Award
Audrey Duncan Major, *Light & Lively Poems, Book II*
Judge Mazebedi, *Chicken Cries Out*
Walt Peterson, *In the Waiting Room of the Speedy Muffler King*
　The 1998 Acorn-Rukeyser Award
Ted Plantos (editor), *Not to Rest in Silence:*
　A celebration of people's poetry
Anna Plesums, *Intrinsic Revelations*
Anna Plesums, *Love and Words*
Al Purdy (editor), *Sing for the Inner Ear*
　The 1997 Sandburg-Livesay Award
Kay Redhead, *The Song of the Artichoke Lover*
Linda Rogers, *Picking the Stones*
　The 1997 Acorn-Rukeyser Award
Margaret Saunders (editor), *Cold Morning*
　The 1997 Herb Barrett Award
Jeff Seffinga, *Bailey's Mill*
Jeff Seffinga (editor), *A Cliff Runs Through It*
Jeff Seffinga (editor), *Ingots*
Jeff Seffinga, *Tight Shorts: haiku and other short poems*
Adèle Kearns Thomas, *Behind the Scenes*
Michael Dylan Welch (editor), *Through the Spirea*
　The 1998 Herb Barrett Award

Non-fiction

James Deahl, *The Canadian Writers' Contest Calendar*
David Allen Greene, *The Script of Under the Watchful Eye*
Claire Ridker & Patricia Savage, *Railing Against the Rush of Years:*
　A personal journey through aging via art therapy

The Sandburg-Livesay Anthology Award

is offered annually. Winners are published in an anthology and cash prizes are awarded. Contest closing is in the autumn; the deadline for 1999 is October 31.

Mekler & Deahl also offers two other contests:

The Acorn-Rukeyser Chapbook Award
for a manuscript of up to 30 pages of poetry

(1999 deadline September 30)

The Herb Barrett Award for short poetry in the haiku tradition

(1999 deadline November 30)

Both offer cash prizes as well as publication.

For full details on these contests, check out our website
www.meklerdeahl.com

or contact

Mekler & Deahl, Publishers
237 Prospect Street South
Hamilton, ON L8M 2Z6

meklerdeahl@globalserve.net
phone (905) 312-1779
fax (905) 312-8285